Undergraduate Writing in Psychology

LEARNING TO TELL THE SCIENTIFIC STORY

THIRD EDITION

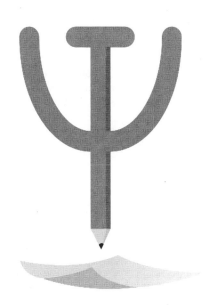

R. ERIC LANDRUM

 AMERICAN PSYCHOLOGICAL ASSOCIATION

Published by
American Psychological Association
750 First Street, NE
Washington, DC 20002
https://www.apa.org

Order Department
https://www.apa.org/pubs/books
order@apa.org

In the U.K., Europe, Africa, and the Middle East, copies may be ordered from Eurospan
https://www.eurospanbookstore.com/apa
info@eurospangroup.com

Typeset in Meridien and Ortodoxa by TIPS Technical Publishing, Inc., Carrboro, NC

Printer: Sheridan Books, Chelsea, MI
Cover Designer: Naylor Design, Washington, DC

CIP data is available from the Library of Congress
Library of Congress Control Number: 2020938088

https://doi.org/10.1037/0000206-000

Printed in the United States of America

10 9 8 7 6 5 4 3 2

*Dedicated to all psychology students learning to write scientifically
and to Allison and Scott, Alyssa and Alex, and my Lisa*

Undergraduate
Writing in Psychology

Undergraduates in psychology, like their graduate student and professor counterparts, need to develop the art and skill of writing that is engaging, clear, honest, and interesting to read. Landrum's gem of a book will help readers to become better writers, and because clear writing is predicated on clear thinking, they will also become better thinkers.

—**Diane F. Halpern,** Past-President, American Psychological Association, and Professor Emerita, Claremont McKenna College, Claremont, CA

The focus on "scientific storytelling" immediately engages students and helps them feel at ease with what, to many of them, may seem a daunting prospect. Whether destined for the workforce or graduate school, students will find Dr. Landrum's emphasis on skills such as planning, attention to detail, and communicating scientific information to be invaluable to their success.

—**Jennifer Thompson, PhD,** University of Maryland University College, Adelphi, MD

The ability to write scientifically is critical for helping students begin to think like scientists. Writing with clarity is an important workplace and life skill. As an undergraduate, I struggled to learn APA Style; the availability of a readable, comprehensive guide like Landrum's *Undergraduate Writing in Psychology* would have saved me from countless hours of frustration. As a gift to my research methods students, I will adopt this book!

—**Jerry Rudmann, PhD,** Professor of Psychology, Irvine Valley Community College, Irvine, CA

Great research + opaque communication = obscurity. The art of science is telling evidence-based stories with mind-absorbing writing. Eric Landrum's guide to scientific storytelling— a true gem from a master teacher—will inspire undergraduate writers with life-relevant lessons about developing their ideas and harnessing the power of language.

—**David G. Myers, PhD,** Professor of Psychology, Hope College, Holland, MI

This is a truly excellent and valuable book. I'm recommending that my institution's writing center, tutoring center, and library reference desk all purchase copies to keep on hand. Dr. Landrum reminds students that writing is all about giving a particular audience a reason to care about their work, as well as understand it. His use of actual drafts of student papers as examples shows students concretely how they can improve their writing.

—**William S. Altman, PhD,** Professor, SUNY Broome Community College, Binghamton, NY

Dr. Landrum's third edition of *Undergraduate Writing in Psychology* is a must-read for psychology students. Because of his welcoming, engaging, and informative tone, both students and faculty will enjoy learning how to write scientifically. His storytelling provides a stage for students to learn and an opportunity to improve their writing. This textbook should be a required reading in many psychology courses.

—**Aaron S. Richmond, PhD,** Professor of Educational Psychology & Human Development, Department of Psychological Science, Metropolitan State University of Denver, Denver, CO

CONTENTS

PREFACE

As you read this book, one of the key points that you will encounter is the importance of writing for your audience. If you are an undergraduate psychology student reading this book, congratulations—*you* are *my* audience! Simply put, I wrote this book for you. Why in the world would I do something like that?

I have to admit that I did not wake up one day and say to myself, "Hey, I think I'll write a book about scientific writing today." Actually, the origin of this book comes from my teaching, especially my undergraduate research methods course. As a student, you take individual courses that accumulate credits into buckets, and as long as you take enough courses to satisfy your institution's requirements, you receive your bachelor's degree. From my perspective, however, these courses can be much more important than that. For example, the research methods course is my opportunity to demonstrate to students how psychologists think, formulate questions, construct answers, and communicate with one another. Your courses should help model the thinking patterns and cognitions of the disciplines you are studying. This book, although primarily about writing scientifically, is also about modeling the process of how psychologists think and express their thinking through their writing.

You have probably already read (or will soon read) your share of journal articles in psychology. As you know, they can be difficult to read and comprehend, but I am telling you that it does not have to be this way. Fundamentally, a well-written journal article is about telling a story, and this storytelling notion is the central, underlying theme of this book. You might not understand every nuance of a journal article or book chapter, but if it is well written, you should be able to extract the gist of the story. My goal in this book is to teach you this scientific storytelling process. It is also important to remember that good stories are not boring, and they stick with us!

Before telling your story, however, you have to do your homework, and this book gives specific examples of how to do that, too. You will find that no matter what area of psychology interests you, being able to write is key. Writing scientifically may seem tedious at times—and let's face it, some aspects of scientific writing, such as formatting your references in American Psychological Association (APA) format—take a great deal of precision and attention to detail. The ability to write scientifically is essential if you want to learn to think like a psychologist! And the ability to pay attention to details can signal the possession of important skills to future employers and/or graduate admissions committees.

Undoubtedly you have many sources of information about writing available to you, such as your instructors, chapters of selected books, the *Publication Manual of the American Psychological Association*, your campus writing center, and so forth. This book is a supplement to all of those sources. It takes some practice to learn to write scientifically, and this book should be most helpful to you as you take those initial steps, particularly because I have modeled the writing process for you, with multiple examples of work from actual students (used with their permission, of course). The more sources of information you have, and the more resources you can call on, the easier and more comfortable you should be as you develop and hone your scientific writing skills.

In the same vein, multiple individuals have been particularly helpful in providing information and resources to help make this book happen. I am grateful to Izzy Riley and Rebecca Cuthbertson, former students of mine who agreed to have actual drafts and final versions of their research methods papers reproduced in this book. Because of their generosity, you get to see actual work in first draft, edited, and revised form. In some cases I have embedded errors that were not there in the first place, just so you could see what those errors would look like and at least one example of how to correct them.

I am especially appreciative of Linda Malnasi McCarter, acquisitions editor at APA Books, who saw value in this project from the very beginning and demonstrated confidence that this book could be a success. Especially with this third edition, she has demonstrated epic patience and undeserved kindness as I was more than slow in making these revisions. I also appreciate the efforts of Beth Hatch, Elise Frasier, Alice White, Robert Kern, and all of the other dedicated individuals and team members who contributed to the improvements and updates to this edition. This book has been revised and updated to comply with the seventh edition of the *Publication Manual of the American Psychological Association* (APA, 2020).

Undergraduate
Writing in Psychology

INTRODUCTION

If you are an undergraduate psychology student reading this introduction, this book is specifically for *you*. Over the course of your undergraduate career, you will be asked to write papers for a number of different psychology classes. Sometimes you will be asked to write a term paper or lab report; other times you may be asked to write a research paper, either summarizing the available research on a topic in a literature review or writing an experimental paper about your own original research. This book is designed to help you write scientifically. One of the features I like most about this book—and I hope you will too—is that it includes actual examples of the different steps involved in scientific writing. For example, when I present the notecard method and software programs for extracting information from sources, you will see depictions of actual notecards. When reviewing how to write the Introduction section of a research paper, you will see an actual student's rough draft, an edited version (as it would be marked by an instructor), and a final draft. In reviewing American Psychological Association (APA) format, you'll see examples of different types of citations you might need to use in your scientific writing.

Although I wrote this book in a linear fashion, you don't have to read it that way. In Chapter 1, I start by establishing the underlying theme of the entire book, that is, that the best communicators in science must be able to tell a good story. As human beings, we enjoy good stories, and we are likely to remember good stories. Chapter 1 provides an overview of the book and briefly reviews the types of assignments for which this book can be most helpful, namely, literature reviews and research papers. The importance of identifying your audience and writing for that audience is presented in Chapter 1 and stressed throughout the book.

Before you can jump in and do any type of scientific writing, careful planning needs to occur, and this is the central topic of Chapter 2. The development of a clear topic and research question (or thesis statement) is essential to laying the foundation on which your scientific writing will be built. I review library search strategies and available resources, and I emphasize the importance of understanding the assignment so you don't waste time or effort writing a great paper that doesn't satisfy the requirements of the assignment.

In Chapter 3, I continue with the next steps of the research process, focusing primarily on identifying key resources and discussing methods for extracting information from those sources. I describe in detail how you can track information from multiple sources that will facilitate the actual writing process and the synthesis of information from your multiple sources.

In Chapter 4, I present some general tips that will apply to most scientific writing in psychology. Key components of this chapter include detailed instructions on creating your first draft, editing, revising, and proofreading. In my discussion of plagiarism, I provide actual examples of text and point out the differences between plagiarized work and sloppy citation methods. This chapter ends with a section on APA Style and format and provides useful information on how to avoid the most common writing errors and tips for improving all kinds of writing, not just scientific writing.

The literature review is a key component of many types of scientific writing. You may be asked to write a stand-alone literature review, or a literature review might be part of a term paper or research paper. Chapter 5 provides guiding principles for writing literature reviews and an actual sample from a former student of mine, including the first draft, an edited version, and the final draft. Seeing actual examples of the process will give you insight into how to improve your own writing.

If you will be writing a complete research paper, then Chapter 6 is essential for you. In this chapter, I review each of the main sections of a research paper (Introduction, Method, Results, and Discussion), again including an actual student sample of each section's rough draft, edited version, and final version. In this way, you can see how an instructor would identify writing problems, and you can also see a student's solutions. By modeling this entire process, I show how psychologists write and think, and, I hope, you will start to internalize and gain those abilities yourself.

Chapter 7 outlines the remaining details of the research paper, including the title page, abstract, references, and tables. In my usual format, I provide examples of each so you can see actual student work.

Although the type of writing you would do for an undergraduate course in psychology is the major focus of this book, scientists also write for other reasons, and Chapter 8 presents examples of other types of scientific writing. An essential component of being a good scientist is the ability to communicate to the larger scientific community, and we often work toward that goal by attending regional or national conferences. As a student, you too might have the opportunity to attend or present at one of these conferences, and thus Chapter 8 opens with examples of writing for an oral presentation at a conference and also provides an example of writing for a poster presentation. However, scientific information is also communicated in other ways, such as writing for blogs and social media. Finally, I close by discussing writing for both pleasure and insight, as there can be beneficial effects of writing for certain medical conditions (as demonstrated in published studies).

You can read the chapters in any order, but if you are actually conducting research for a psychology paper, I suggest you read Chapters 2 and 3 before you start writing your research paper. If you are writing a term paper that is mostly your opinion, I would suggest Chapters 1 and 4. If you are in a course such as research methods or experimental design, then I would recommend that you read all the chapters in sequence so you can see the process from start to finish. You will note that in many places I have used information from the internet to provide cogent examples. In Chapter 3, I present a section titled "Evaluating Sources," and I have followed the advice I present there in my selection of materials from the internet. As I have been, always be careful about referencing information from the internet, and ensure that the information and its source are credible and reliable.

It is my sincere hope that the ideas I present will help you with your scientific writing. If you can think of anything that I can do to improve this book, please email me (elandru@boisestate.edu). Your suggestions are both welcome and valuable, and in future editions of this book I will be able to add resources to improve my advice to undergraduate psychology students.

1

Why Psychology Students (and Not Just English Majors) Have to Write

Give me a dozen healthy infants, well formed, and my own specified world to bring them up in, and I'll guarantee to take any one at random and train him to become any type of specialist I might select—doctor, lawyer, artist, merchant, chief, and, yes, even beggarman and thief, regardless of his talents, penchants, tendencies, abilities, vocations, and race of his ancestors.

—JOHN B. WATSON, *BEHAVIORISM*

Have you ever tried to read an article in a scholarly journal and discovered that you understood very little of it? Scientific writers in psychology often develop poor writing habits; as one author put it, they exert "a corrupting influence on young scientists—on their writing, their reading, and their thinking" (Woodford, 1967, as cited in Van Wagenen, 1991, pp. 2–3). As an undergraduate student, you are in a position to recognize these corrupting influences and put an end to poor scientific writing! Scientific writing need not be dull or boring, as you can see from the chapter opening quotation. For a lab report, your instructor may require a slightly more cautious tone than the one John B. Watson (1925) used in this excerpt from his book *Behaviorism*, but then, part of becoming a good scientific writer is learning that how you want to present your message—be it in a scholarly article, popular book, website, blog, or talk at a conference—affects the level of formality you use.

Scientific writing in psychology can be a difficult task because of its complexity. Like other complex skills, writing improves with practice, instruction, and feedback. Although writing scientifically for psychology requires some specialized skills, it also shares important characteristics with other types of writing with which you may already be familiar. The goals of this book are to help you become more confident in your ability to write scientifically and to help you improve your scientific writing skills.

7

There are different approaches to categorizing writing assignments, and it is important to note that scientific writing is not the "best" type of writing or the most valuable type of writing but just one method of writing that allows the author to attempt to achieve specific goals. One classification system lists six major types of writing: expository, descriptive, persuasive, poetic, technical, and narrative (Copywriting in Action School, 2019). Even though we place lab reports, literature reviews, term papers, and research articles in the "technical writing" category, remember that scientific writing shares characteristics with other types of writing. Scientific writers are expressive, exploring topics in new and different ways, working to inform the reader, clearly placing the topic in a research context, and persuading the reader to accept the results as presented. Thus, scientific writing is not an independent form of writing separate from other approaches, but it may be thought of as a particular writing style that follows specific rules and tells a story in an objective yet clear, definitive voice. One way to build your confidence in your own scientific writing is to think of it as just one of several possible ways to approach telling a story.

TELLING A GOOD STORY WITH SCIENTIFIC INFORMATION: CAN IT BE DONE?

Even though it may not seem so in the psychological materials you read (textbooks, journal articles, websites, book chapters) and write (lab reports, literature reviews, term papers, research papers), good scientific writers tell a story. This idea of storytelling, even in psychology, is not new (e.g., Roediger, 2007; Salovey, 2000; Silvia, 2007; Trochim, 2001). However, not all scientific writers achieve the goal of good storytelling, as you can attest when you read a journal article and come away with no idea what it was about. The characteristics of good storytelling in literature also apply to good storytelling in scientific writing. For instance, much of the advice that Ballon (2005) gave to screenwriters also applies to scientific writers. For example, in writing a screenplay, Ballon advised the writer to start with a topic or issue, relate the beginning to the ending, and hook the audience. Screenwriters are taught to develop a conflict and flesh out the relationship between protagonist (hero) and antagonist (villain). Scientific writers do the same, but not so dramatically. In testing the relationships between independent and dependent variables, other forces such as nuisance variables or confounds (antagonists) come into play that threaten the veracity of our conclusions. Screenwriters are also taught to write in a three-act structure, with Act I as the exposition, Act II as the complications, and Act III as the resolution (Ballon, 2005). Scientific writing follows a similar storytelling sequence, although the areas of emphasis for screenwriters and scientific writers are different. Screenwriters even have their own script format that must be followed, with formatting and layout rules and specialized terminology, like a slugline (the instruction as to the setting for the screenplay's action, written in the script in capital letters). Scientific writers also have specific rules to follow in the presentation of new scientific information. Good writing tells a compelling story, whether it be a screenplay or scientific journal article.

A similar analysis of the elements of storytelling is offered by Appelcline (n.d.). She lists five tools of good storytelling: setting, character, plot, backstory, and detail. Interestingly, this summary of the elements of storytelling comes from an undergraduate student discussing online gaming (sometimes, a story is a story is a story!). The elements of storytelling are universal, and each of these elements is an important component of scientific writing in psychology.

First, the character: What is the story about? Have you ever walked out of a movie theater confused about what the movie was about? The main character of the story must be clearly defined, or else we have problems following the story. In scientific writing, the "who" or the "character" may not be a person but a behavioral variable or phenomenon of interest. The main character may be the effects of depression or the variables that predict career satisfaction. But if the variables are not clearly defined or the hypotheses are not carefully stated, we may have trouble following what the scientific story is all about.

Second, the backstory: What happened in the past that leads us to the present? Screenwriters and storytellers are adept at "filling in the blanks" and providing context for us to understand the story's dynamics, how the conflict unfolds, and how that conflict is ultimately resolved. Scientific writing places a high value on the backstory, as seen in stand-alone literature reviews or literature reviews contained in term papers or research papers. The backstory is important in scientific writing because it provides the context of why one would bother to study a particular psychological phenomenon. And the backstory helps tell scientists what we already know, so we can focus on studying what we don't know.

Third, the plot: What is happening now? For the screenwriter, this would be Act II, or the complications. But for scientific writing, the plot is revealed by the sequence of items presented to the reader. Background information is followed by current events (such as the Method section and the Results section in an experimental paper), which are followed by outcomes and then interpretation of outcomes. Scientific writing describes what happened in the past, what is happening now, and what might happen in the future. As you can see, scientific writing is very linear and does not use common dramatic storytelling conventions like flashbacks or foreshadowing. But any good story needs a good plot; otherwise the reader has a hard time caring about the story.

Fourth, the setting: Where is the story happening? In a good story, place, time, weather conditions, and other elements of the setting make it possible for readers to experience the narrative. Sometimes elements of the setting serve to move the action forward. Scientific writers use the Method section of their journal article or lab report to show where and how an experiment happened. If it seems relevant, they may tell more about the setting, such as the time the experiment took place, the conditions in the room, the instructions given to participants, and so forth. Scientists want to get a clear idea of the setting so they can understand the context in which a particular process took place and particular results were obtained—this is extremely helpful if other scientists want to replicate (repeat) the study.

Fifth, the details: What specific items should the audience notice? Screen-writers and storytellers have numerous tools available to them to communicate to the audience, and with time and experience, they learn which are the most effective in a particular situation. The more you write scientifically, the more experience and confidence you will build. Scientific writing in psychology is very specific about the requirements that must be provided to the reader. The seventh edition of the *Publication Manual of the American Psychological Association* (APA, 2020) prescribes many of the requirements that scientific writers must satisfy. It also offers guidance on writing clearly and concisely. The chapter on bias-free language guidelines, in particular, encourages students to write about people with inclusivity and respect, and it promotes use of the singular "they." However, it does not focus on helping you become a better scientific storyteller, and sometimes students feel at odds with this goal when constrained by the conventions of APA Style. The *Publication Manual* thus differs from this book, but the two resources complement each other. Furthermore, having a preor-dained format may be more of a benefit than you think. Silvia (2007) described it this way:

> Writing a journal article is like writing a screenplay for a romantic comedy: You need to learn a formula. As odd as it sounds, you should be grateful for APA Style. Once you learn what goes where—and what never goes where—you'll find it easy to write journal articles. (pp. 78–79)

Silvia's advice applies to many types of scientific writing you'll be doing as an undergraduate psychology student.

WHY DO WE TELL THE SCIENTIFIC STORY?

Clear communication using the elements of storytelling allows the writer to create a story in such a way that it will be memorable to others. Ultimately, the most important reason for scientific writing in psychology is communication to others. The primary audience is usually professional psychologists or psychol-ogy students, but not always.

Many areas of psychology are indeed quite complex, but if readers with some technical knowledge of psychology have difficulty comprehending at least some aspect of a piece of scientific writing, then the author has failed in their goal to communicate. But writers may be writing for different audiences, some of which may be surprising to you, and sometimes the multiple audiences are at odds with one another with respect to the desire for clarity in the writing. Sometimes psychologists write to impress other psychologists, and unfortu-nately, sometimes scientists have a tendency to equate plain language with oversimplification. Sometimes psychologists write in the same manner they were taught in graduate school, following the examples of their mentors, and sometimes psychologists write to obtain promotion and tenure. Although the goal of scientific writing should be the clear communication of ideas, in reality scientific writing is often sidetracked by goals that do not always promote clarity. The importance of writing as a method of communication is made clear in an important policy document called the *APA Guidelines for the Undergraduate Psychology Major, Version 2.0* (APA, 2013). In this document, a national task force (of which I was a member) developed and refined goals from the earlier effort (Version 1.0). Out of the five overarching goals for psychology majors, Goal 4 (see Exhibit 1.1) centers on communication, and Goal 4.1 specifically addresses the desire for psychology majors to be able to demonstrate effective writing for different purposes (APA, 2013).

There is nothing wrong with scientific writing serving multiple goals, as long as clear communication is the utmost goal. There are many other motivations for writing. For instance, Gottschalk and Hjortshoj (2004) reminded us of the various types of informal writing, especially student writing. Writing can be used to inform, to learn, and to prepare for performance (see also H. L. Miller & Lance, 2006). Teachers use writing assignments, such as beginning-of-semester questionnaires, written evaluations, and 1-minute papers, to obtain students' feedback on teacher performance. Teachers also use writing to help students learn by having them write reflection journals, participate in email discussions,

---

EXHIBIT 1.1. Goal 4: Communication—Foundational and Baccalaureate Indicators

4.1. Demonstrate effective writing for different purposes

Foundational indicators: Students will	Baccalaureate indicators: Students will
4.1a Express ideas in written formats that reflect basic psychological concepts and principles	4.1A Construct arguments clearly and concisely based on evidence-based psychological concepts and theories
4.1b Recognize writing content and format differ based on purpose (e.g., blogs, memos, journal articles) and audience	4.1B Craft clear and concise written communications to address specific audiences (e.g., lay, peer, professional)
4.1c Use standard English, including generally accepted grammar	4.1C Use grammar appropriate to professional standards and conventions (e.g., APA writing style)
4.1d Write using APA Style	4.1D Employ APA Style to make precise and persuasive arguments
4.1e Recognize and develop overall organization (e.g., beginning, development, ending) that fits the purpose	4.1E Tailor length and development of ideas in formats that fit the purpose
4.1f Interpret quantitative data displayed in statistics, graphs, and tables, including statistical symbols in research reports	4.1F Communicate quantitative data in statistics, graphs, and tables
4.1g Use expert feedback to revise writing of a single draft	4.1G Seek feedback to improve writing quality resulting in multiple drafts

Note. Adapted from *Guidelines for the Undergraduate Psychology Major: Version 2.0* (p. 30), by the American Psychological Association, 2013 (https://www.apa.org/ed/precollege/about/psymajor-guidelines.pdf). Copyright 2013 by the American Psychological Association.

and answer study guide questions. In one study based on the sixth edition of the *Publication Manual*, researchers found that although students learn from reading the *Publication Manual*, screencasts are more efficient for instructors and may be more palatable for students (Fallon et al., 2018). Based on these findings, the researchers concluded that screencasts should be combined with applied assignments. Teachers also use writing to help students show what they know, for example, by using a rough draft–revised draft process in which students begin to understand the importance of a first draft in leading to a desirable final result.

TYPES OF ASSIGNMENTS

Even within scientific writing for psychology, there are myriad types of writing assignments. H. L. Miller and Lance (2006), in a review of the literature, identified 12 types of writing assignments used in psychology: progressive papers, multiperspective papers, group papers, reflective writing, portfolios, interpretative writing, short writing, literature reviews, written feedback, reaction papers, knowledge maps, and student newspapers. Although I do not provide detailed instruction about each of these types of assignments, the basic ideas of style and editing and construction will provide helpful assistance for many, if not most, of these writing assignments. I focus more closely on two of the most common (and perhaps most difficult) types of scientific writing in psychology: literature reviews and research papers. Whereas different types of scientific writing are briefly previewed here, in later chapters I delve more deeply into the mechanics of assignments, with examples, and demonstrate the writing techniques that can lead to success.

Lab Report

At many colleges and universities nationwide, laboratory (lab) sections accompany the coursework in a particular area. In psychology, you might encounter a course in cognitive psychology or physiological psychology that has an associated lab section in which students conduct mini experiments and are asked to write lab reports summarizing the session's results. For example, in a lab associated with a human memory course, students may be asked to "experiment" on themselves and collect data based on the phenomenon being studied. An instructor could present students with a series of words based on the Stroop effect. Students are asked to say the color of the ink, not the word (but the words are actually color names). The experimenter records how much time elapses between the presentation of words and their utterance, and the number of erroneous colors named (both dependent variables). Students in the class would then be asked to prepare a laboratory report. One benefit of the lab report is that it allows the instructor to determine the extent to which the student understands the hands-on exercise in the lab.

Entire books are devoted to the development of research skills using a laboratory approach in psychology (Crawford & Christensen, 1995; Langston, 2002). However, most lab reports are actually miniature versions of a complete research paper (University of Richmond, n.d.). Thus, the sections of a research paper—title page, abstract, Introduction, Method, Results, Discussion, references, and tables or figures (if necessary)—would most likely be the sections of your lab report, only in a condensed version. You may find that your instructor wants a modified version of the above, with sections such as title, Purpose, Materials, Procedure, Observations and Data, Analysis of Data, and Conclusions.

Literature Review

In some cases, a literature review might share some of the components of a lab report, but it is also often part of the first section of a term paper or research paper. *Literature* is a fairly generic term, meaning the available published works on a particular topic—including journal articles, books and book chapters, internet sources, and more. A researcher conducts a *literature* search using tools like APA PsycInfo and Google Scholar (more on those later) with the goal of finding research articles that can be used in a number of contexts. First, a student could write a review of the literature. This would entail an integrated synopsis or summary of some aspect of the psychological literature related to a variable or behavior of interest. In addition, the literature review is often a key component of the Introduction section of a research paper or lab report. Furthermore, depending on the type of term paper assignment, a review of the literature could be a key part of a term paper. Simply put, a literature review is a review of materials available on a particular topic, examining the most relevant, recent, and scholarly work in an area.

Literature reviews are usually centered around a conflict or controversy, presenting both sides by organizing all the relevant studies in a coherent manner, or by selecting just one point of view and compiling studies that support it (University of Washington, 2017). Simply put, a literature review is your scholarly review of the available information about your topic, up-to-date, and organized in such a way that tells a coherent story for the reader. A literature review is an integrated resource that both analyzes and synthesizes the literature into a coherent and current status report. A well-written literature review is valuable to the reader because it presents a comprehensive summary of previous work, providing a context for present and future work. This may be why components of literature review strategies are found in many types of scientific writing, including lab reports, term papers, and research papers. In fact, sometimes literature reviews are published as stand-alone text, called *review articles* (University of Washington, 2017).

Writing a literature review involves (a) formulating the problem or topic to be examined, (b) searching the available literature for relevant and topical work, (c) evaluating the literature and its appropriate contribution to providing a context to previous work, and (d) analyzing and interpreting the pertinent literature (Lyons, 2005). A well-written literature review is useful because it integrates the research of others; identifies similarities, differences, and trends in previous research; demonstrates a comprehensive knowledge of the topic; and exemplifies analysis and synthesis skills in the evaluation of reviewed materials. Given the academic benefit of literature reviews, it is no surprise that literature reviews are frequent components of writing assignments.

Term Paper

To be honest, *term paper* is such a generic phrase that it is difficult to summarize an exhaustive set of rules for every term paper. A term paper could be almost any type of assignment, including a reaction paper, a semester-long journal, an opinion paper, or an argument–debate paper (H. L. Miller & Lance, 2006). Perhaps what distinguishes a term paper from other papers is that (a) it is prepared outside of class and (b) it is whatever your instructor says it is. In this context, I'll refer to a term paper as a nonexperimental research paper—a paper in which original research is not being reported, like a summary of others' research findings. Typically, your instructor would assign a term paper to (a) help increase your expertise in a particular subject area and (b) help sharpen your analytic (critical thinking) and writing skills (McGraw-Hill Higher Education, n.d.). Writing improvement takes practice, and term paper assignments help provide that practice, giving the instructor some insight into your level of understanding of a particular subject or topic.

Because term papers are such a versatile writing assignment, they are used widely, but the requirements by discipline (and even within the same discipline) may also be widely different. Be sure to clarify key issues with your instructor, such as desired length, use of APA format, overall goals of the assignment, references versus works cited versus bibliography, and so forth.

Research Paper

The research paper is where the details of an experiment are presented formally. One of the reasons why experimental research papers are so important in psychology is that they model the thinking processes that psychologists use. That is, as effective storytellers, we provide a character (topic to be studied), backstory (literature review), plot (hypotheses to be tested), setting (where and how the experiment was conducted), and detail (participants, materials, and procedure). Research papers resolve the preexisting conflicts between the previous literature and the current findings at the end of the paper, just as the screenwriter resolves plot conflicts in Act III. Research paper assignments, like most academic writing assignments, share the goals of teaching students how to read like a psychologist as well as how to write like one (McCormick, 1994).

MEETING AUDIENCE NEEDS: WHAT IS THE INSTRUCTOR ASKING FOR?

Even though an instructor may have multiple goals for a writing assignment, to be successful in your scientific writing as a college student you must ultimately remember this: Give the instructor what they want, or as Sternberg (2005) said more eloquently, write for your reader. Let's explore that in a bit more detail.

Writing Maxim: Write for Your Audience
(Or, Give Your Instructor Exactly What They Want)

This means that you should completely understand the nature of the writing assignment before beginning your writing. Although an instructor may say to prepare your assignment using "APA format," do they mean all the rules (strict adherence) or most of the rules (less strict adherence)? It is essential that you ask the instructor what they want in any type of writing assignment, or else you risk investing a great deal of effort into a writing assignment that may not turn out the way you expect. When they said "APA format," did they mean sixth- or seventh-edition rules? Did they mean strict seventh-edition rules even though they said to use single spacing because that is their preference (which means that technically it is no longer seventh-edition APA format)? However, be careful not to become too cynical—sometimes this is a fine line to tread. With some instructors, you may have to play the game and pretty much give them what they want, but with other instructors, you'll explore your world of ideas and practice expressing those ideas scientifically. Perhaps the corollary to the writing maxim should be "Know Your Instructor." This is excellent preparation for the workforce, by the way, because nearly all of us work for or report to someone, and being able to figure out what your supervisor wants is a good skill to have.

This also means, however, that instructors need to be clear in communicating their expectations to students! You might ask your instructor if they have a grading rubric available for your review (see my example in Chapter 4). Sometimes, even when the instructor says "Write in APA format," it may not be as simple as that. The *Publication Manual* (APA, 2020) recommends one space after a period at the end of a sentence, but what if your instructor says to use two spaces because they think sentences are easier to read with more separation between them? The moral of the story is this: Even though an instructor might tell you they want term papers prepared in APA format, be savvy enough to ask whether they have any personal preferences or exceptions that might not be apparent. Do ask your instructor if they are using a rubric; there is good evidence that when students use a rubric on APA writing assignments, their performance improves compared with students not using a rubric (Greenberg, 2015; Obeid & Hill, 2018).

Sternberg (2005) offered four suggestions for achieving the goal of writing for your reader. First, make sure you use vocabulary appropriate for the reader. Even though you may be writing for your college professors, you may be presenting a topic to them outside of their own expertise. If you find yourself using highly specialized terminology, be sure to either define it or present it in a context in which the definition can be understood. In other words, "eschew obfuscation." This saying comes from legendary editor and Furman University professor Dr. Charles Brewer, who often gave this advice to faculty members submitting manuscripts to the journal *Teaching of Psychology*. "Eschew obfuscation" is a clever way of communicating the idea to seek out clarity and avoid writing in a confusing manner. Good scientific writing communicates clearly. Thus, it is better to say "write clearly" than "eschew obfuscation" because the goal is for the reader to understand your writing, ideally without frequent use of a dictionary.

Second, maintain the appropriate level of formality for the writing situation. Writing an anonymous 1-minute paper on a 3-in. × 5-in. notecard at the end of class is much different from handing in a research paper you have worked on all semester/quarter/term. Scientific writing tends to have a high level of formality because of the objectivity desired in the message. Students sometimes slip into conversation mode in their writing, for example, "Now I'll talk about the process of synaptic transmission." Although a good scientific writer wants the reader to become engaged with the topic, scientific writing is not a conversation between writer and reader. But wait! Throughout this chapter (and throughout this book) I have been referring to "you" and "us"—that isn't APA format, is it? It is not! I am not writing this book in APA format, even though parts of this book are about APA format. Rather, I'm writing this book for you, in hopes of connecting with you and expressing my ideas about writing scientifically. I too must know my audience, and in this case, I'm writing this book to students and for students.

Third, include only those details that are relevant to your audience. When writing for your instructor, you will probably not need to define terms like *independent variable* and *dependent variable*, but you might have to define such terms if you were writing for a broader audience, such as the general public.

Finally, avoid abbreviations. Not only can they be distracting, but an editorial in *Nature Neuroscience* ("How Experts Communicate," 2000) makes the point that unfamiliar abbreviations make additional demands on memory and that "clear writing reduces the demands on working memory by presenting information where readers expect to find it" (p. 97). Using an abbreviation should make the work of the reader easier, not the writer. If you cannot avoid abbreviations, then use them sparingly. As the *Publication Manual* (APA, 2020) suggests, to be effective, the item being abbreviated should be used at least three times after its introduction (and when introducing the item, always spell it out the first time unless the abbreviation is accepted as a word).

WHY APA STYLE AND FORMAT EXIST

In the early 20th century, there were only a handful of journals in the social sciences, and journal editors determined the shape and content of published works. As scholarship in the social sciences developed, the number of journals and articles in these disciplines proliferated. Inconsistency in reporting standards and in basic layout of content led to confusion among researchers and other authors and consumers of scientific literature. A standard format began to appear in the 1890s, thanks to Joseph Jastrow at the University of Wisconsin (Blumenthal, 1991). As an alternative to long essays in early psychological journals, Jastrow suggested that "minor studies" be published by stating a problem and describing the research methods used, followed by the findings, data analysis, and a conclusion. Jastrow's imprint on scientific writing in psychology is still with us today.

In 1928, editors and business managers of psychological and anthropological journals met and discussed the typical format and information that a published journal article should provide. In a 6½-page article published in *Psychological Bulletin* in 1929, Bentley et al. provided suggestions to guide authors in their preparation of manuscripts. This guidance was organized into four main sections: (a) general form of the manuscript, (b) subdivision and articulation of topics, (c) references and footnotes, and (d) tabular matter and illustrations. These guidelines were revised again in 1944, but expanded to 32 pages, and the first *Publication Manual* was published (as a separate volume, not appearing in *Psychological Bulletin*) in 1952.

Subsequent editions of the *Publication Manual* included more detail, which added to its page length as well; the seventh edition (APA, 2020) is 427 pages long. Some writers have suggested that the *Publication Manual* is overly prescriptive and rule based (Vipond, 1993). The *Publication Manual* is indeed more of a guide to a style of scientific writing than simply a specification of the format in which to present scientific information, and this style and format is used not only in psychology but in a host of other disciplines, including social work, education, nursing, business, and coaching. Moreover, the seventh edition of the *Publication Manual* provides much more flexibility in interpreting APA Style, a change resulting from many years of feedback from students and focus groups.

Reading a paper prepared according to APA format may not be overly entertaining, but the linear presentation of ideas and events enhances the objectivity and formality to which science ascribes. Although research is not always conducted in a linear fashion, there is a linearity to the general thought process. Generally, a scientist comes up with an idea and researches the background of that idea, yielding testable hypotheses. They then conduct a study to test those hypotheses, followed by analyses to determine whether the hypotheses were supported or refuted. The scientist then discusses the general meaning of the work, concluding with the limitations of the study and suggestions for future work. The linear thought process of the scientist is reflected in the linearity of APA format and the structure of scientific writing. When the work is written to be shared with others, it is framed in this linear sequence. Just like good storytelling, as discussed earlier in this chapter, understanding character development and backstory provides a context in which to appreciate the plot and the resolution of the character conflict. Scientific writing provides the same backstory and character development so that the plot can be resolved, but the plot centers on psychological ideas and behaviors rather than people.

This linearity of presentation may seem boring to some, but after some experience in reading psychological literature, you begin to expect the sequence and appreciate it. It provides a structure and framework common to scientific thinking and work and makes sense to scientists. Have you ever watched a movie in which the storyline is presented out of sequence? Some movies like to use flashbacks as a creative device to assist in dramatic storytelling. When flashbacks are used too much, it becomes hard to follow the story and make sense of what is happening. I find myself thinking, "Is this now or then?" rather than fully comprehending the story. As scientists, we aspire to not let the structure and framework of the story detract from the story itself.

Later portions of this book delve more deeply into the details of APA format for our different types of writing assignments. In fact, although I refer to the rules of writing as APA format, it actually refers to a style of writing (see https://apastyle.apa.org/). Vipond (1993) referred to this APA Style of scientific writing as *plain style* and suggested three main elements: clarity, literal writing, and brevity. Writing in a clear and orderly style promotes clarity, which is also associated with logical and smooth writing. *Literal writing* prefers a straightforward approach for the presentation of ideas while avoiding a creative approach to writing, such as the use of literary devices (e.g., alliteration, rhyming, poetic expressions, clichés). Writing a research paper is a complex task, and a number of resources exist, such as websites and resource books. However, the ultimate guide for the preparation of research papers in psychology is the *Publication Manual* (APA, 2020; 7th ed.). Although you can learn a lot about writing from reading the *Publication Manual*, it's not designed to teach writing. The goal of this book is to help you become a better scientific writer. Many of the guides available for writing research papers help to interpret the complex APA Style and formatting rules, and this book also provides concrete examples of how to navigate through the complexity of APA format. But before starting your first scientific writing assignment, there is much work to be done—we need a foundation on which to build. Both planning and researching are essential foundational components of successful scientific writing, and we turn to these next.

2

Starting Your Paper
Finding the Thread of Your Story

I have a vast deal to say, and shall give all this morning to my pen. As to my plan of writing every evening the adventures of the day, I find it impracticable; for the diversions here are so very late, that if I begin my letters after them, I could not go to bed at all.
—FRANCES BURNEY, *EVELINA*

Although in a different context, the author of this opening quote sounds just as busy as today's college student. There are so many different demands on students that finding the time to complete writing assignments is hard enough; thus, this chapter is about the planning processes that should precede your scientific writing in psychology. Assignments may differ widely across your various psychology and social sciences courses. This writing approach will make it easier to complete your assignment and increase the chances of earning a better grade.

SELECTING A TOPIC

For some assignments, your instructor will provide the topic. For others, you'll be given a range of topics to write about, and sometimes the topic can be nearly anything. Before you start writing, even before you start researching, you need to seriously consider your topic and plan out how you will treat it in your paper. The plan may be very brief, such as for an opinion paper, or it may be fixed, such as for lab report. By "plan," I don't necessarily mean a complete outline, although outlines can be extremely helpful. Planning in this context means not only selecting a topic but also knowing the direction you are taking, including the goals of your writing (and maybe a quick database search too). Your writing goal could simply be to clearly communicate ideas (although this is not so simple), to demonstrate to teachers what you know, to learn, to acquire a skill, or to prepare for performance (such as rough drafts). In the last chapter of this book, I'll address other types of writing and their purposes as well.

Obviously, you will want to select a topic that will allow you to successfully satisfy the instructor's requirements or learning outcomes for the writing assignment. When students are given a wide range of possible topics, the level of "freedom" is sometimes daunting because you might be torn between writing about what you want to write about versus writing about what you think your instructor wants you to write about. If you are unsure, ask the instructor in class or in a discussion board post, or ask privately in an email or during office hours. Odds are, if you are wondering about a question, someone else in the class has the same question, too! If the possible topic pool is broad, here are some ideas (modified from Landrum & Davis, 2020; Martin, 1991) on how to generate topics to write about, especially research topics.

Observation

Looking at the world around you may give you some great ideas to write about. Sometimes just sitting on a bench at the mall or in the park can present ideas about human behavior that could be fascinating to think about and write about. Given that I ride the elevator six floors up and down on a regular basis, I see all sorts of elevator behavior that would be fascinating to write about (yes, I know I should take the stairs more often). You can obtain good topics to write about just by observing the world you live in.

Vicarious Observation

Perhaps someone told you about a situation or an event they witnessed and you found it hard to believe—this would be an example of vicarious observation. Another example would be reading a famous study in your psychology textbook and wondering whether those results would apply today. You can get good ideas from others' thoughts and observations as well as from your own.

Expand on Previous Ideas

Perhaps in an earlier class you wrote a literature review or a term paper on a particular topic but did not have the opportunity to conduct the study—that could be a source of a topic to write about. Or you may have heard an instructor hypothesize about a "what-if" situation, but you were hard-pressed to believe the hypothesis. Previous ideas are a good source of writing topics. You may have had an interest in a topic for some time but never had the chance to explore it while in college—expanding on your own previous ideas can also be a good source of topics.

Focus on a Practical Problem

I often suggest that students pick a topic to write about that, if they had all the time in the world, they would write about anyway. In other words, try to find a topic that can help you answer a real question that you have—completing the assignment and doing the writing are much more pleasurable when you are studying something of personal interest. I once had a student ask me about the impact of withdrawals ("Ws") on her transcript because she was thinking of applying to graduate school. I didn't know the answer, so that became a great topic for us to study (Montoya et al., 2000) and resulted in a published research paper[1] (Landrum, 2003).

These are just some of the ways in which you might think about selecting a topic to write about, especially if the topic is not determined for you by your instructor. Although I've outlined some good sources for getting ideas, Sternberg (2005) listed a number of mistakes that students can make when selecting a topic, including (a) selecting a topic that is not interesting to them, (b) selecting a topic that is too easy or too safe, (c) selecting a topic that is too difficult, (d) selecting a topic with inadequate literature available, and (e) selecting a topic that is too broad. In some cases, you may not be able to select your own topic, so you may or may not be interested in what you write about. However, if you do have the opportunity to choose a topic, choose one in which you have an intrinsic interest. Sometimes students select a topic that is too easy or too safe, such as writing about a topic they have already written about in another class. If you think about doing this, be sure to check with your instructor to see whether this is OK—in some cases, you may be accused of plagiarizing or cheating if you "double dip," or use one paper for two different purposes (I'll clarify this later in Chapter 4 in the section on plagiarism). On some campuses, professors may compare the work you submitted electronically against a data-base of all previously submitted work at the institution—including your own work in previous courses. Submitting work again from a previous course without permission could be considered self-plagiarism—again, it is vital that you check with your instructor before you "recycle."

Another benefit of planning is giving yourself an adequate amount of time to complete the assignment with the best chances of success. This means you should always quickly peruse the literature, including what is available through your library, before committing to a writing topic. Although you may want to write about a challenging topic, and learn about the topic in the process, you do not want to choose something too difficult. If it is a particular subspecialty in psychology, the vocabulary may be too steep to learn in time to write a coherent paper. Selecting a topic with inadequate literature could mean that very little has been published on the topic, or only a limited amount of literature will be available in the time you have to complete the assignment. Your library can

---

[1] How did it turn out? A single withdrawal from any class did not seem to have a substantial impact for most respondents. Withdrawals hurt a student's prospective graduate school admissions chances when there were multiple withdrawals in courses like research methods and statistics.

order journal articles and books for you, but depending on their availability, you may not be able to access them in time.

Finally, sometimes students select a topic that is much too broad, such as "children who are depressed." This topic is much too broad for a lab report, term paper, or research paper and would require a literature review of volumes and volumes. In later chapters, I'll present more ideas on how to narrow your topic appropriately, but don't forget the most valuable resource for topic selection—your instructor! Your instructor wants to read a good paper and wants you to learn from the writing assignment, so they are motivated to help you get off to a good start by selecting an appropriate topic. Once the topic has been determined, the next step (depending on the assignment) may be to formulate either a thesis statement or a research question.

DEVELOPING A THESIS STATEMENT OR A RESEARCH QUESTION

You may be familiar with the term *thesis statement* from a previous English composition course. In fact, some of your psychology professors may instruct you to write a term paper using a thesis statement (although a thesis statement would be used much less frequently in a lab report or research paper). See Table 2.1 for examples of thesis statements. The thesis of your paper is the topic that you are writing about plus a specific assertion about that topic (Online Writing Laboratory, n.d.). Brunsvold (2003) offered a more complete description of what a thesis statement is and what it is not. A thesis statement

- is an assertion, not a statement of fact;

- takes a stand, rather than introducing a topic;

- is a main idea, not a title;

- is narrow rather than broad, and is specific rather than general; and

- makes one main point rather than several main points (several main points may be difficult for the reader to follow).

Brunsvold (2003) suggests that a thesis statement should be a complete sentence explaining, in some detail, the topic you are writing about. Following our maxim, if your instructor requests a thesis statement, be sure to provide it in the format and manner requested.

In a more typical type of psychology writing assignment, you may be asked to provide a research question rather than a thesis statement. A good research question is critical to successful scientific writing in psychology. A coherent and well-formed research question will help guide the rest of the research process, helping you to determine what information is and is not relevant to your writing assignment. Depending on the type of writing assignment, your research question will be essential if you are developing testable hypotheses, such as for a research paper or research proposal.

TABLE 2.1. Thesis Statement Examples

Not so good	Better
It is a fact that individuals who are more liberal do a better job recycling.	The degree to which a person chooses to recycle may be related to their political beliefs.
Researchers who rely on survey methodology are unaware of the disadvantages of response rate, lack of anonymity, and cost per respondent.	Survey outcomes need to be considered in the context of the limitations of survey research methodology.
Homelessness is unfair to children.	Children who are homeless are at risk to experience multiple deficits in their cognitive development.
The effect of student study time on classroom performance.	The effectiveness of student study strategies is influenced by more than time on task.

Some of the characteristics of a superior thesis statement also apply to the development of a research question. For instance, your research question should not be too broad, but it should also not be so narrow that the research is not doable within the constraints of the assignment or the task—a little bit like the fable, the goal is not too warm, not too cold, but just right. The examples in Table 2.2 show a balance between what is too broad and too narrow in creating a research question.

After you have formulated your thesis statement or research question, evaluate it—ask yourself the "so-what" question. Let's say your paper topic is about recycling. If you were to ask yourself the so-what question, you would ask "So what about recycling?" You should be able to provide a compelling answer to why recycling is important and why writing a paper or doing research about recycling is also important. Ask your instructor whether they care about your topic or whether their response is "So what?" More importantly, ask yourself

TABLE 2.2. Research Question Examples

Too broad	Good balance	Too narrow
Why do adolescents smoke?	What is the impact of peer smoking on an adolescent's decision to smoke or not?	If an adolescent's parents are divorced (one parent has remarried and one parent has not), and if one of those parents smokes, does the adolescent begin smoking sooner?
Does marriage make a person happy?	What is the relationship between age at marriage, marriage longevity, and marital satisfaction?	What is the best combination of exact ages for two people to be married and also be happy for most of the time married?
How can students improve test scores?	What is the association between cumulative student study effort and test performance?	If a student studies 2 hours before the test, and another 2 hours the day before the test, will the student perform well?

the so-what question. If you have control over the topic you write about, try to select a topic you are passionate about and have an intrinsic interest in so that you can answer the so-what question with ease. For instance, if you have just been told that one of your grandparents has Parkinson's disease, you might choose to do your paper about that topic. If you can write about topics of interest, it becomes a win-win—you satisfy the requirements of the assignment and you learn about something that interests you.

If the answer to your so-what question is "nobody cares," try to find another way to spin your topic into a more relevant thesis statement or research question. If your thesis statement is "Parkinson's disease causes a lot of pain to many individuals," it is difficult to get excited about because it is so dry. However, "One in every 272 Americans who reaches age 65 is likely to suffer from the multiple debilitating effects of Parkinson's disease" is much more persuasive and compelling (note that this example is completely made up). When students or colleagues ask me about my research, I tell a pretty convincing story about why the topic is important to me. In fact, if I cannot tell a good story, then I should think about why I am doing that research in the first place! If you are doing research, either for a paper or as a research assistant, you too need to be able to persuasively tell your research story to others. Practice making that 3-minute elevator pitch with confidence. The ability to tell a compelling and persuasive story can be helpful for your future in numerous ways, ranging from self-confidence in a job interview, to competence in an area important for success in graduate school applications, or even to an advantage when applying for undergraduate research grants. When departments hire faculty members, interviewers ask prospective faculty about their program of research, and they should be excited about it and able to communicate it clearly. When you go home for your holiday break and someone asks about your research paper, you too should be able to describe your work in a compelling fashion.

UNCOVERING THE BACKSTORY, PART 1: YOUR LIBRARY SEARCH STRATEGY

The final part of this chapter presents some general thoughts about your strategy to find supporting information for your scientific writing assignment. I present specific details in the next chapter, but here I give some ideas about how to organize and plan your search strategy before you implement it.

APA PsycInfo is an incredibly useful database for beginning research on almost every topic possible in psychology. APA PsycInfo is published by the American Psychological Association, and it is offered through a number of vendors. You will need to look into the database collection at your college or university library to see whether you have access to APA PsycInfo. As of January 2020, the APA PsycInfo database contained nearly 4 million records, covering 2,290 journal titles, publications from 50 countries and 29 languages (APA, n.d.-b). For current information on APA PsycInfo coverage, visit the APA website (https://www.apa.org/pubs/databases/psycinfo/?tab=1). If you are searching for psychological literature, including journals, books, or even dissertations, APA PsycInfo is most likely the best place to start. In fact, the reference materials cataloged in APA PsycInfo range back centuries, with reference book materials available from the mid-1800s (APA, n.d.-b). Figures 2.1a and 2.1b show examples of APA PsycInfo search screens. The look and feel of the system at your institution may be different, depending on the delivery platform your campus uses. As you can see, there are multiple options in conducting your APA PsycInfo search. The first screen is just the starting position. It is usually best to select "Advanced Search" because that will expand the number of search parameter boxes from one to three. Following are some factors to help facilitate your search and to reduce the number of relevant articles ("hits") to a manageable number.

First, you'll have to make some decisions about your search terms. This is perhaps the most important step of the entire process! The database uses a specific vocabulary. For instance, if you were to search on the term "depression," your search would have different results than if you searched on "depressing," "depressive," or even "depressed." Thus, to search effectively, you have to be specific in what you are instructing the database to search for. Sometimes the most difficult decision is determining what search term to use. For instance, if you were writing a term paper, would you search on "manic-depressive disorder" or "bipolar disorder"? The APA has published the *Thesaurus of Psychological Index Terms* (Gallagher, 2007; print version). There is also an online version available with a 2019 update (https://apa.org/pubs/databases/training/thesaurus). This resource is devoted to helping researchers identify the correct terms for

FIGURE 2.1a. Example of APA PsycInfo Search Screens

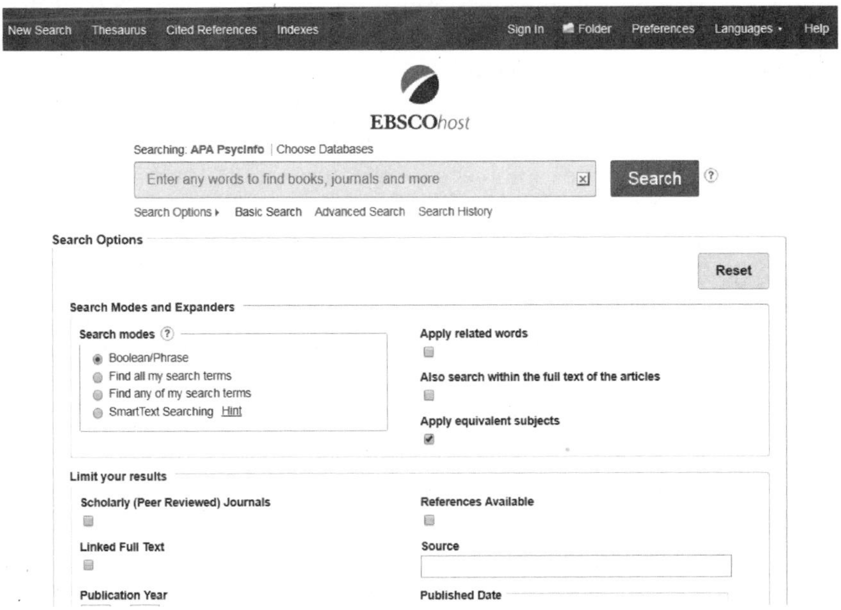

FIGURE 2.1b. Example of APA PsycInfo Search Screens

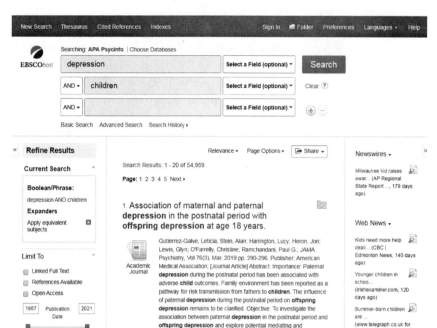

searching databases, and it offers very helpful suggestions for narrowing or broadening your search. A sample search for different keywords or search terms is achieved with the thesaurus feature; a sample record using the term "depression" is presented in Figure 2.2.

In addition to searching for keywords (which the thesaurus is invaluable in identifying), in APA PsycInfo you can also search on many other fields, such as author, title, and publisher. Another search feature in APA PsycInfo and many other databases is the use of Boolean operators, such as AND, NOT, and OR. For instance, conducting a keyword search on "depression AND children" will give you results with those keywords (see Figure 2.1b for this actual search with the results from January 2020). Searching on "depression OR children" will broaden the search and return all the index entries referencing depression or referencing children, without necessarily overlapping. A search on "depression NOT children" will narrow your search, including records on the topic of depression but excluding those records that report "children" in the keywords. A different method of broadening the search is called *truncating*. In truncating, the database searches for records containing the fragment of the keyword you provide. So, instead of searching on "depression AND depressing AND depressed AND depressive," by truncating you would conduct a search for "depress*." The

FIGURE 2.2. Example of APA Thesaurus of Psychological Index Terms Search Screen

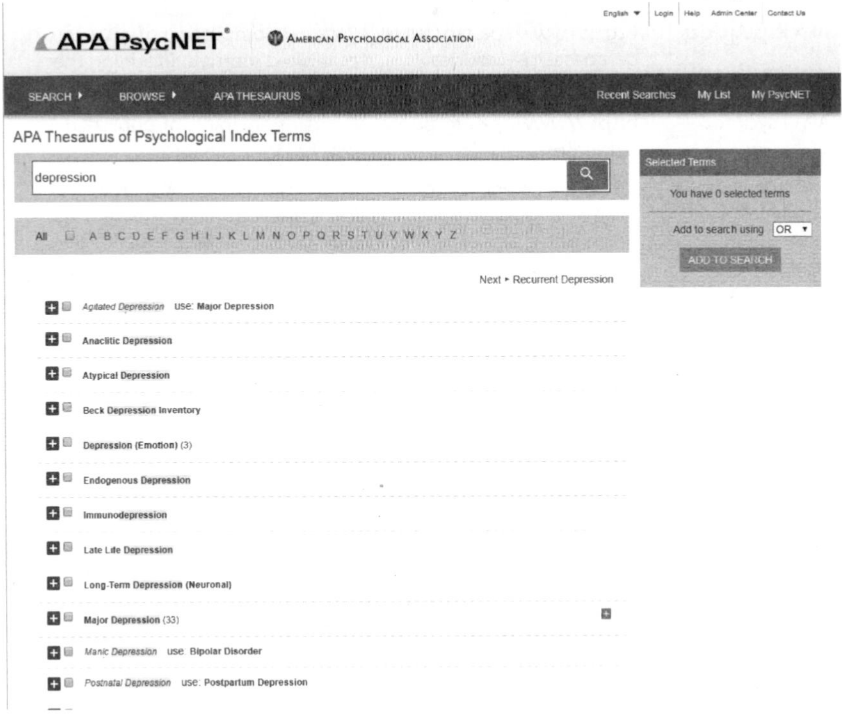

asterisk, called a *wildcard,* locates any record that starts with "depress," no matter how the word ends. This search would also find records you might not expect, such as records using the keyword "depressive."

In addition to APA PsycInfo, there are many other places to find valuable psychological information. Table 2.3 provides some additional helpful resources that you may want to consult in addition to your APA PsycInfo search. Note that some of the websites listed may only provide information about the database, not access to it. You should ask your instructor or a librarian for more information about what databases are available to you at your college or university.

For most scientific writing in psychology, APA PsycInfo is the best place to start. Its versatility allows for subject, keyword, and author searches, making it a very powerful tool. However, there is one other very powerful search tool, which seems to be less known to students—Web of Science. Using the Web of Science citation search feature, you can discover where and when a previously published work has been cited in other published works. This is a powerful tool for following a line of research from an early, seminal article through to today. Let me give you an example. Say your assignment is to write a literature review on cognitive dissonance theory. You discover that this theory originated in 1957 when Leon Festinger wrote *A Theory of Cognitive Dissonance* (you could have discovered this through an APA PsycInfo search, from your social psychology

TABLE 2.3. Examples of Online Resources

Name of database	Website	What it covers
APA PsycArticles	https://www.apa.org/pubs/databases/psycarticles	Full-text compilation of APA published journals, including the ability to browse tables of contents.
APA PsycInfo	https://www.apa.org/pubs/databases/psycinfo	Contains abstracts of published psychological literature.
ERIC (Educational Resources Information Center)	https://www.eric.ed.gov/	Provides abstracts of educational literature with full-text access via ERIC Document Reproduction Service.
MedlinePlus PubMed	https://medlineplus.gov	Contains abstracts of articles from sources that publish biomedical research.
Web of Science	http://www.wokinfo.com	A high-level subscription-based service that allows for database searches based on author, citation, journal, and other fields.
APA PsycExtra	https://www.apa.org/pubs/databases/psycextra	Gray literature indexed from a psychological perspective. Includes full-text documents for 70% of the records, including technical reports, position papers, and conference presentations.
APA PsycBooks	https://www.apa.org/pubs/databases/psycbooks	Provides access to APA books, out-of-print texts, and classic texts. Includes an electronic version of the *Encyclopedia of Psychology.*
APA PsycTests	https://www.apa.org/pubs/databases/psyctests	A database of psychological measures, surveys, and questionnaires; typically research-focused and not commercially available measures.
Google Scholar	https://scholar.google.com	A search engine that allows access to more scholarly sources of information, often providing direct links to accessible information.

Note. Data from Kidd et al. (2000) and McCarthy and Pusateri (2006).

instructor, or even from the social psychology chapter of your introductory psychology textbook). Then you discover that Festinger published a journal article about the subject even before that, in 1954. The Web of Science database will allow you to see who has cited Festinger (1954) since its publication (see Figure 2.3a for sample search). An example of the results is shown in Figure 2.3b. As it turns out, Festinger's book and his paper titled "A Theory of Social Comparison Processes," published in the journal *Human Relations* in 1954, are very popular; according to the Web of Science database as of January 2020, he has been cited in 7,494 other publications.

FIGURE 2.3a. Example of Social Sciences Citation Index Citation Search

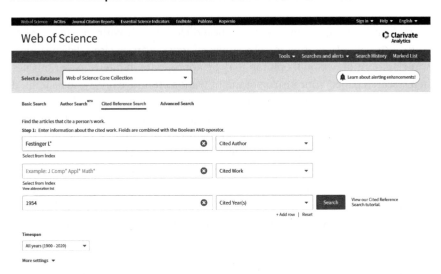

Note. From Web of Science, by Clarivate Analytics, 2020 (http://www.wokinfo.com). Copyright 2020 by Clarivate Analytics. Reprinted with permission.

FIGURE 2.3b. Example of Social Sciences Citation Index Citation Results

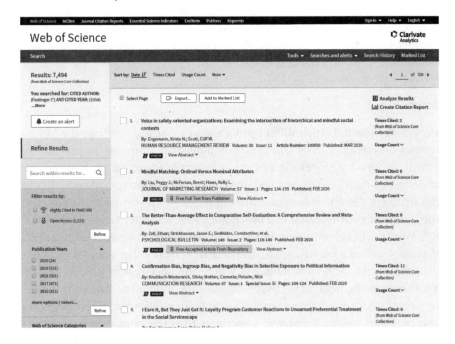

Note. From Web of Science, by Clarivate Analytics, 2020 (http://www.wokinfo.com). Copyright 2020 by Clarivate Analytics. Reprinted with permission.

WHAT SOURCES ARE ALLOWED?

As part of the planning process, you should clarify with your instructor what sources are allowable, that is, what types of works can be cited. For instance, some amount of personal opinion may be appropriate in a term paper but not in a research paper. Your instructor might want a literature review to be limited to published journal articles and books, not internet sources. This is, however, more complicated than it may seem. Some journals publish print editions and also publish the work electronically on the internet. Some journals only publish electronically and never publish a "paper" copy. There are also citation rules about an "advance online publication," that is, an article that has been accepted for publication by a journal and released electronically but is not yet available in print (this can get complicated very quickly). Is it allowable to cite auxiliary electronic content from an article when that content does not appear in the print edition? Be sure to clarify this before you begin your research so you don't waste time and effort.

You may also want to inquire about the relevance of popular sources versus more academic sources. Would it be appropriate to include information from magazines such as *Psychology Today* or *Scientific American*? You may be tempted to use Google and Wikipedia as sources, but I recommend you check with your instructor first. Do the articles you cite in your paper need to be peer reviewed? If you're looking for other sources of credible information, you may want to explore APA PsycExtra (https://apa.org/pubs/databases/psycextra/), a database that covers materials disseminated outside of peer-reviewed journals. It includes technical reports, conference proceedings, and other difficult-to-find publications.

Journals

How does a journal article differ from a magazine article? Perhaps the fundamental difference is how the article is published. Journals in psychology operate under a peer-review system in which manuscript submissions are reviewed by multiple referees (experts) before a decision is made whether or not to accept the article for publication. Let's say that you wanted to publish the results of your research in a psychology journal. After selecting the journal, you would submit the manuscript to the editor. As a general rule, you may only submit a manuscript to one journal at a time. The editor sends your manuscript out for review, which is where the peer-review process begins. Your peers in the field (other psychologists) are asked to review your manuscript and decide whether or not it is suitable for publication. These peers are also called *referees*, and you will sometimes hear the phrase "refereed journal" (which means the journal follows this peer-review process). Reviewers are often individuals with prior success in publishing their own manuscripts. By the way, reviewers are not paid for this task, and it is considered to be providing service to the discipline.

How does an individual reviewer evaluate a manuscript? Of course, this varies across journals and individuals, but in general, scholarship is the key. For the manuscript to be considered scholarly, there should be a thorough review of the literature, a keen grasp of the subject matter, concise writing, adequate research skills, demonstrated importance of the work to psychology, and an understanding of the journal's readership (the journal subscribers).

Reviews are often done anonymously, meaning the writer is unaware of who the reviewers are. Sometimes journal article submissions are masked, meaning the reviewers also do not know who the author is. Authors can request a masked review, or sometimes it is a journal's policy to mask review all submissions. This procedure is used in an effort to be as fair and objective as possible and to give full consideration to the contribution a journal article can make to the larger body of scientific knowledge.

Magazines and Other Popular Sources

The peer-review process required for journal publication differs from that for a magazine in that a magazine pays people to write articles. Authors of journal articles are not paid and are sometimes even asked to help defray some of the publishing expenses. Although magazine articles may be checked for accuracy, they do not undergo the scrutiny and examination that journal articles do. The majority of journal articles are well documented with supporting references that note when an idea has been borrowed from elsewhere. A magazine article is rarely as extensive in documenting the author's academic and scholarly work. One other minor difference between the two is that journals are typically not available for purchase at bookstores and are subscription-based, whereas magazines are typically available at newsstands or bookstores. In addition to magazines, there are, as you already know, numerous other outlets for information, including newspapers, television, radio, wikis, blogs, podcasts, and so forth. Remember to ask your instructor if you are unsure about what potential sources of information are allowable for your writing assignment.

Gray Literature

Gray literature refers to documents not commercially available (e.g., via a book or a journal) that may be of value but also may be difficult to authenticate and verify (Mathews, 2004). This is information not under the control of commercial, professional publishers. APA provides a gray literature database called APA PsycExtra, which includes documents such as research reports, policy statements, annual reports, standards, videos, conference papers and abstracts, fact sheets, newsletters, pamphlets, directories, popular magazines, white papers, and grant information (APA, n.d.-a). Items in APA PsycExtra do not overlap with items available in APA PsycInfo and APA PsycExtra is a fee-based service (check to see whether your library subscribes to APA PsycExtra). You may be able to find many of the same items in APA PsycExtra through your own internet search, but the benefit of APA PsycExtra is that it is organized, indexed, and updated monthly, and more than 70% of the items in APA PsycExtra have full-text links (APA, n.d.-a). But be careful—just because an APA PsycInfo or APA PsycExtra search result contains a full-text link does not mean that the article is of higher quality; it just means that it is more convenient for you to obtain. *You* still must determine whether the resource is relevant to your writing assignment.

Now you need to put your library search strategy into action. Once you start turning up resources that might be useful, you'll need to ask yourself, "Is this resource useful? How do I extract the most relevant information from each resource? How do I keep track of all the bits and pieces of information I am extracting from the literature?" The next chapter aims to help you answer these questions.

3

Extracting the Useful Nuggets From a Literature Search

Moreover, the most painstaking and laborious research, covering long periods of years, is necessary in order to accumulate the material for any history worth writing at all.
—THEODORE ROOSEVELT, *HISTORY AS LITERATURE*

In this chapter, I strive to demystify the literature search and the processes of analyzing and synthesizing the research literature; however, it would be irresponsible of me to claim that these processes are anything short of painstaking and laborious, as noted in the opening quotation. I hope you will find that by putting considerable time into a well-organized literature search, you will save time when it comes to composing the paper, hopefully resulting in a better grade. Scientific writing relies on the presentation of facts, theories, and hypotheses in an impartial and objective manner to the furthest extent possible. Scientific writing generally strives to avoid the personal opinions of the writer and attempts to test the validity of ideas. A major component of this approach is the ability to incorporate evidence, specifically research-based evidence, into the written product. Chapter 2 ended with an organizational plan for finding relevant information for your scientific writing project; in this chapter I address implementing that search strategy, evaluating possible sources, and analyzing and extracting information from those sources.

UNCOVERING THE BACKSTORY, PART 2: PRIMARY AND SECONDARY SOURCES

An effective search strategy begins with the organizational foundation presented at the end of Chapter 2. Knowing your keywords and exhausting relevant databases are important first steps. Next comes the actual research, evaluating sources, and extracting and analyzing information. You will, as much as possible, want to retrieve primary sources. What are primary sources? A primary source is an original document. For example, if you read a journal article about original research and the article was written by the researcher, that is a primary source. If you read about the original research, but what you read was not written by the original researcher but instead appeared in another journal article or a textbook, that would be a secondary source. Essentially, authors cannot control how others interpret their work—they can only control what they write. As scientists, we prefer primary sources whenever possible. This gives us the opportunity to understand the writer's perspective as opposed to someone else's perspective about what they thought the original writer meant.

In the previous chapter, I detailed a number of databases from which you would typically obtain leads about the research available on the topic you are writing about (e.g., APA PsycInfo, Web of Science, APA PsycExtra, Google Scholar). Here I highlight other resources and avenues you might pursue in implementing your search strategy.

Online Catalogs

After you've conducted your database searches, you'll need to know what is available at your library. There should be an online search engine through your local library that will help you identify available resources. To obtain resources that are not available at your library, you may need to look into interlibrary loan options.

Magazines

Magazines can often be a good source of ideas for topics to write about, and a magazine article may give you tips on primary sources to find. In general, however, you will typically not be citing magazine articles in scientific writing.

Journals

Journals are often the preferred "currency" of scientific writing. Because of the rigorous standards of refereed journals, their credibility is highly valued. Journals are also preferred because of timeliness—the information in a journal article is more current than that in most books and textbooks (secondary sources).

Newspapers

Similar to magazines, newspapers may be a good source of ideas to write about and may lead you to the original, primary resources. If you want to demonstrate that your topic is an important matter in today's world, citing a source from a newspaper article might be a good strategy in the opening paragraphs of a literature review. But unless your scientific writing assignment is about a current event, you will not often be citing newspapers.

Reference Books

Reference books can be a wonderful resource of secondary sources that provide original references and interpretations of others' work. They can also provide citations to key or seminal works in a particular field. Your introductory psychology textbook may well be one of the most useful reference books you own because it covers a wide range of topics in psychology.

Books

Books, especially those that are primary sources, can be quite valuable in scientific writing. Books give an author the opportunity to expound in greater detail on a particular theory or how variables interact in a complex fashion. Books are not typically as up-to-date as journal articles because of the increased lead time necessary to publish a book. You will also sometimes encounter edited books, in which each chapter is written by a different author. These edited books can be extremely valuable in your search for sources because they often provide multiple and diverse perspectives on some aspect of the same problem or topic.

Internet Sources

There are a number of internet search engines (such as Google and Google Scholar) available that can help you uncover research related to a paper topic. Internet searches may lead you to original, primary resources or to secondary sources. When retrieving information from the internet, take care to evaluate its source (which is often difficult to determine). Later in this chapter, I present some standards for evaluating research sources from any medium.

Knowledgeable Faculty

Don't forget about your department faculty! Depending on the course, your instructor may have expertise on the topic you are writing about. Other faculty members in your department or program are also likely to know something about your topic or may at least be able to point you in the direction of additional primary and secondary sources.

Reference Librarians and Library Search Strategies

A reference librarian has special talents that can be particularly useful to you as you use the library to obtain the research necessary for your scientific writing assignment. A reference librarian is someone who is educated and trained to help others locate reference materials (and they can do much more). At larger schools, there may be a reference librarian specifically for psychology or the social sciences. Don't overlook this valuable resource on your campus.

In addition to the numerous research strategies presented, I have found that students often implement a systematic library research strategy (Landrum & Muench, 1994). In a study of such strategies, I identified four specific approaches that students use for library research: (a) person-specific strategies, in which students build self-confidence and library skills; (b) library-specific strategies, in which students learn what is available to them and how to use their library; (c) paper-specific strategies, in which students learn to understand the details of writing a paper and how library resources can help them; and (d) reference-specific strategies, in which students learn how to use journal articles and books in the library. I point out these library strategies because your research and writing approach may differ, depending on the type of class, type of instructor, or even type of assignment. Adapt to the needs of the assignment. For instance, in a history of psychology class, the emphasis may be more on classic works, focusing on books; however, in a social psychology class, your instructor may want the latest research published in journals. Not only may your strategies be course specific, but they may also be instructor specific. Try to find out what types of sources your instructor prefers. In my research methods course, I want students to focus mainly on journal articles because they tend to be the major currency in experimental psychology. Our writing maxim from Chapter 1 also applies to types of research sources.

EVALUATING SOURCES

Once you've completed your library search and gathered (or at least examined) possible research and other sources for your paper, and before careful analysis and extraction of information, you'll need to determine the value or validity of the sources you've gathered. This can be a very important part of any scientific writing assignment, and development of this skill is valuable for any future that psychology majors pursue. For some types of information, evaluating the veracity of a source is easy. Because of the peer-review process, we have confidence in articles that are published in scholarly journals. Books published by reputable, well-known sources also allow for confidence in the information they present. For other sources, however—such as information from the internet—evaluation is crucial. I suggest you consider the following three evaluative areas when examining sources, suggested in part by Harris (2005).

Authorship and Expertise

Authorship is an essential consideration when using a source for a scientific paper. Sometimes the information may come from a website, brochure, or pamphlet, and authorship is difficult to ascertain. This is a problem. If no one is willing to "own" the information, how valuable can it be? To determine the author's expertise, you must know who they are. The author may be a corporate entity, which is fine, but authorship should be acknowledged so that you can understand the original source of the information and any particular point of view or bias that the author may have.

Currency and Timeliness

Depending on the type of paper you are writing, currency may be important. If you are writing a literature review of the developments in an area of social psychology in the past 10 years, then timeliness of your sources is obviously an important concern. If you are writing a term paper about some school of thought in psychology's historical development (e.g., structuralism), then the currency of information may not be as important in evaluating sources.

Accuracy and Corroboration

On the basis of what you have read from other sources, are the findings presently accurate and without bias? Does a new or controversial idea put forth by an author place that idea in the context of previous literature? Is corroboration possible with the ideas presented—for example, have others considered this idea or have replication studies on the topic been completed? Are the sources of the ideas documented by a knowledge of previous work?

When extracting information from the internet, it is essential to evaluate each source using these standards. Once you are confident that a source is valid, then it's time to critically read the source and extract information you might use in your own scientific writing assignment.

WHICH INFORMATION IS MOST PERTINENT?

You've done your research and gathered sources that you believe are valid and that you think will be helpful for your paper. It's now time to begin critically reading and analyzing your sources so that you can decide what pieces of information may be pertinent to your writing assignment. There is no right or wrong way to do this, and there are numerous approaches. The key is to structure the way you gather information to facilitate its use in your paper. If you organize your ideas beforehand, composition will seem easy. Having a method of note-taking allows you to scan through many potential sources systematically; then, when you integrate multiple sources from your research, your paper will show signs of scholarly writing. The difference between a good paper and an excellent paper is often the level of synthesis. Chances are that when you feel that you've exhausted the literature and know your topic inside and out, you will do a good job of synthesizing research for your paper. By using the note-card method (or some variation of it), writers can organize their thoughts and ideas beforehand rather than while they are writing.

Here I present an extended example of how to take notes and transition into composing the paper: the notecard method. This method involves noting single ideas on 4-in. × 6-in. index cards and coding those ideas to their sources, which are noted on 3-in. × 5-in. index cards. This method can be adapted to a number of different computer applications and still be tactile (i.e., if you print out your notes and physically shuffle their order), or it can be entirely paperless. A number of computer-oriented alternatives to the notecard method are summarized at the end of this chapter—and I'll present a modified version of the notecard method that you can use with Google Sheets.

Step 1: Select a Paper Topic

Try to generate a topic that interests you, but keep within the confines of the instructor's assignment. The challenge is to select as specific a topic as possible for which there are library materials readily available.[1] Try to decide on a paper topic after examining what your library has to offer. This approach allows you to make sure that there are adequate resources available before you are totally committed to a topic.

Step 2: Create an Outline

Sketch an outline of the major points you want to make in your paper. Again, this step should be done after looking at the available library materials. You may already know what points you want to make, but the quick library search may give you more ideas. Try to be as concrete and specific as possible in your outline. With certain types of scientific writing, your outline may already be prepared for you (Introduction, Method, Results, and Discussion).

Step 3: Make Reference Notecards

On 3-in. × 5-in. index cards, create your reference list or bibliography. Place only one reference on each card, and in the upper right corner give each refer-ence a code (A, B, C, etc.). This code will link each idea card (discussed next) to its source. Write each reference in American Psychological Association (APA) Style (more information about APA reference format is provided in Chapter 4).

---

[1] In certain classes I make students approve their paper topic, and if they want to change topics, they have to have the new topic approved. Countless times I have approved new topics, and the reason the student wanted to change their topic was that "there is no research readily available on the original topic I proposed."

The *Publication Manual* (APA, 2020) has very specific reference formats, and book references are formatted differently than journal references; be sure to note the differences. Writing the reference notecard in APA format saves you time later when you type the reference section, and including only one reference per card makes it easy to alphabetize your references. For examples of what a reference notecard might look like, see Figures 3.1, 3.2, and 3.3. (Note that the cards presented in the figures are not to scale.)

FIGURE 3.1

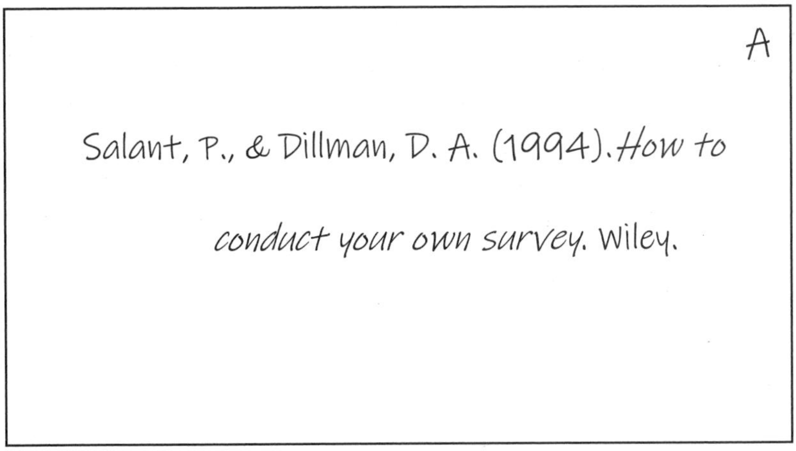

Here's a 3-in. × 5-in. reference notecard, not to scale. Notice how the reference is already in APA format, with hanging indent, double-spacing, and even the attempt to write in italics. This is a book reference.

FIGURE 3.2

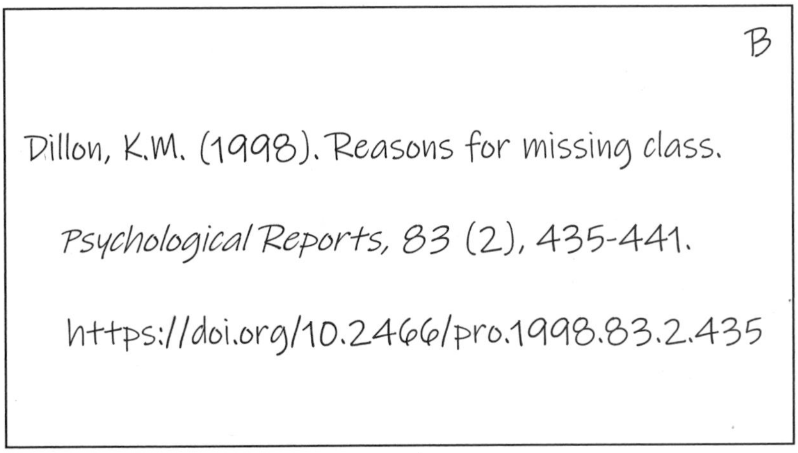

Here's another reference notecard. This one is from a journal article. It is as close to APA format as can be handwritten, including the journal name and volume number in italics.

FIGURE 3.3

> C
>
> Williams, R.L., & Eggert, A. (2002). Notetaking
>
> predictors of test performance. *Teaching*
>
> *of Psychology, 29*(3), 234-237.

Here's one more example of a reference notecard, this time for a journal article with two authors. Note the ampersand (&) rather than the word "and."

Step 4: Make Idea Notecards

On 4-in. × 6-in. index cards, take your notes on each source or reference you have selected. On each card, write only one idea that you think you might use in your paper (later on, this will facilitate the organization of your paper). For Reference A, you may have four separate ideas you might incorporate into your paper, and you would label them A1, A2, A3, and A4, respectively (see Figures 3.4 and 3.5 for examples of idea notecards). If you think you might like to use the idea in a direct quote, be sure to note the page number on the idea notecard (see Figures 3.6 and 3.7).

FIGURE 3.4

> A1
>
> The number of people who complete the survey compared to the number of people you ask to complete the survey is called the response rate.

This is a 4-in. × 6-in. idea notecard (not to scale) from Reference A. Put only one idea on each notecard. This idea is a paraphrase from the book cited.

FIGURE 3.5

> C1
>
> These teaching strategies help students take better notes: pausing, repeating critical points, using visual cues, and taping lectures for later review by students.

Here's an idea notecard from the reference in Figure 3.3 that summarizes the original idea in the journal article.

FIGURE 3.6

> B1
>
> "Faculty and students had significantly different opinions as to the acceptability of 46% of the reasons given for missing class. Yet faculty were often reluctant to confront the students directly."
>
> p.440

Here's an example of an idea notecard from the reference in Figure 3.2, but this is a direct quote. Note the exact page number in the bottom right corner of the notecard. You'll need to cite this page number in the text of your paper.

FIGURE 3.7

> C2
>
> "The independent variables include two notetaking domains (reading and class lectures) and three dimensions of notetaking (completeness, length, and accuracy)."
>
> p.235

One more example of an idea notecard; again, this is a direct quote with the page number recorded for later use. Also remember that you don't have to use the direct quote; you could turn this idea into a paraphrase, but you must still give credit to the original author.

Step 5: Plan the Paper

Before you actually begin writing the paper, plan its course. With your revised outline and your idea notecards, organize your paper by selecting ideas (note-cards) and grouping them together. Place your idea notecards in the order in which you are going to use them. How do you know the order? Your outline (Step 2) is your general road map. Try to integrate the ideas as much as possible (i.e., don't discuss all the ideas from Reference A, then Reference B, etc.). The whole point of this system is to help you synthesize (integrate) similar ideas from different contexts.

Step 6: Write the Rough Draft

Now it's time to actually start writing the paper. Of course, you've already done much of the writing, which has helped you to become very familiar with your reference materials and the points you want to make. In later chapters, we'll revisit this topic as I present specific guidelines and suggestions for writing lit-erature reviews and research papers. Following your paper plan, write the text by using the notecards you've already organized. You need to make the text readable, providing the necessary transition between ideas. A reference list is typically not required with a rough draft (it normally appears at the end of the paper), although you should cite your sources in the text using APA format. Also, be sure to include a title.

Now, write the rough draft. You can literally "lay out" your paper by arrang-ing the idea notecards paragraph by paragraph. With the citation noted in the upper right corner, you can go back and add proper citations later. On a desk or table, spread out the cards so you can "see" your paragraphs—this is why I like the paper notecard method better than the Google Sheets variation. Although the Google Sheets approach allows you to do this electronically, it is difficult to "see" the entire view all at once (see Figure 3.8). Think of each of the columns as paragraphs in your Introduction section, and perhaps the individual cells or boxes are sentences. Exhibit 3.1 shows what it might look like if you mapped your Introduction to notecard citations after it was written.

See if your instructor will review your rough draft without assigning a grade. If that's not an option (and it may not be in larger classes), ask one of your classmates to read your paper. If you're not sure about something you want to write or an argument you want to make, try it; the worst that can happen in

EXHIBIT 3.1. Mapping Your Introduction to Notecard Citations

	C3			A7; J3; B14	
	B6	D5		I4	
	A2; E1	D4; C6	B6		
A4	H3		A4		
B7	A5		C1	K3	A9
F2		J1	H1		

FIGURE 3.8

PSYC 321 Idea Notes

File Edit View Insert Format Data Tools Add-ons Help

Share

	A	B	C	D	E	F
1	**Instructions**	Provide the complete APA reference for the article that you are taking notes on.	In Columns C through whatever, take "notes" on the item you placed in column B. Only one idea per cell. If you think there are 10 usable ideas in a source, you should type those ideas individually in 10 separate cells. When you read the next item, you might determine that there is nothing "usable" in that source after all. That's OK; just leave the citation and go onto the next. Think ahead – you will need to cite at least six sources in your Introduction section, due February 20.			
3	Example	Tucker, J. R., Hammer, J. H., Vogel, D. L., Bitman, R. L., Wade, N. G., & Maier, E. J. (2013). Disentangling self-stigma: Are mental illness and help-seeking self-stigmas different? *Journal of Counseling Psychology, 60,* 520-531. doi:10.1037/a0033555	Self-stigma is when people internalize stereotypes and take in negative public attitudes and apply those attitudes to themselves.	People associate seeking psychological treatment with the terms "awkward, old, defensive, dependent, insecure, unsociable, not in control of one's emotions, and weak or disturbed" (p. 521).	Modified Labeling Theory is the idea that once the label is applied, the person who has received the label starts to also apply all of the negative attitudes, traits, and qualities to himself/herself.	The independent variable was the two group comparison (distressed students vs. mental health patients) and all of the measures on symptoms and scales were dependent variables.

Example of how Google Sheets could be used to record ideas from a source, simultaneously tracking the reference information.

the draft stage is that you receive some free advice. If you see a lot of red ink or many track changes comments on your returned draft, think of this too as free advice (and on the topic of advice, don't forget about the resources available at your campus writing center). Remember, the rough draft is not the final version; the comments should help to improve your paper. At some point, we all need outside consultants to help us improve and sharpen our skills.

Quite frankly, the notecard method works. By reading, understanding, and analyzing your sources to extract information, taking notes on those sources, and then using those notes in writing your paper, you become better acquainted with the topic. Your understanding of what you are writing about becomes deeper and less superficial.

KEEPING TRACK OF IDEAS

Essentially, there are three different strategies to use when you are taking notes on your sources—quoting, paraphrasing, and summarizing (Harris, 2005; University of Maryland University College, 2011). Harris (2005) offered a number of situations for using a direct quotation from another source in your own work: expert declaration (a quote from an authority figure), direct support, effective language (the elegance and clarity of the author's words), historical flavor, specific example, controversial statement, or material for analysis. Direct quotes should be used sparingly, and you should be careful to adhere to the instructor's assignment guidelines. For example, when I teach research methods, I tell students they cannot use more than three direct quotes in their formal research paper. I do this so students will realize that scholarly writing does not involve a string of quotations; rather, it involves the interpretation and communication of ideas in the proper form (the ability to translate complex scientific ideas and communicate them in your own words is a valuable and marketable skill). A string of direct quotations in a paper essentially means that other authors "wrote" your paper for you.

You should use a direct quotation when an author has said something so eloquently (i.e., effective language) that a paraphrase or a summary would lessen the meaning or impact of the original statement. When you are recording your idea notecards, if you think you might use a direct quote, write it down on the notecard, and note the page number from the original source. If the source does not have a page number—such as a website—then record as many details as you can, like the paragraph number or the section of the website where the quotation occurs. In APA format, the use of a direct quotation requires that you provide the page number (or in some cases, paragraph number or location) from the source. Also, if you use a long quote (40 words or more), APA format requires that the quote must be indented in the text. One last concern about quoting is that you should not quote from one source too often (Harris, 2005), especially if the goal of the assignment is for you to integrate and summarize previous research. Quoting (or even citing) the same source repeatedly shows a limited review of the literature or synthesis of ideas from multiple sources.

A paraphrase is very different from a direct quotation in that it is a translation of the writer's original words into your own words, using roughly the same number of words (Harris, 2005; University of Maryland University College, 2011). Paraphrasing is seen as more scholarly than using direct quotes because it demonstrates a deeper understanding of the original work; in fact, it is quite a talent to be able to take others' ideas and convert them into a less complex or more clear form (this is an important part of what good teachers do). Paraphrasing allows you to reword, simplify, or clarify the original writer's meaning. When using the notecard method, most of your idea notecards should be paraphrased.

A summary is similar to a paraphrase in that you translate the author's original words into your own; however, a summary is shorter than the original (Harris, 2005). Key benefits of summaries include simplifying and condensing the author's original ideas. Summaries are also a good strategy when you are extracting information for your idea notecards.

Whether you are using a direct quote, paraphrase, or summary, the key benefit in connecting your idea notecards to your reference notecards is to give credit where credit is due. This is critical in scientific writing, and failure to do so is plagiarism (discussed later), which can have serious repercussions.

KEEPING TRACK OF SOURCES

The references that you gather using your reference notecards (or Google Sheets or other software program) are more important than you might think. A reference list shows off your "academic pedigree"; that is, it shows the line of thinking and research that you followed to place your current work in its proper context. Your instructor will know how much effort you put into your writing assignment by examining the extent of the references you have cited. The reference list should be meticulously prepared (note that there are various rules in APA format for the different types of materials you might cite). In later chapters I review the proper preparation of reference citations in APA format.

In other courses with a writing component, you may be asked to prepare papers or reports using Modern Language Association (MLA) format. MLA format is commonly taught in high schools and in college-level English classes. Unfortunately, MLA format differs vastly from APA format, although some of the underlying goals of scholarly writing are the same. One significant difference between MLA and APA is in the use of references. In APA format, when you cite a reference in the text, you use the author's last name (or names, if there are several authors) followed by the publication year. In MLA format, the author's name is usually followed by the page number in the original source from which the information was taken. In APA format, there is a References section at the end of the paper that lists every reference cited in the main text of the paper. At the end of a paper in MLA format, you might have a works cited page, including frequent notations like *ibid.* and *op. cit.* If you were preparing a bibliography (or works consulted page), it would list every reference article you consulted, whether or not it was cited in the text of the paper. As always, be sure to heed your instructor's advice and use the referencing method that they prefer.

Maximizing the Notecard Method

It may appear that the notecard method involves a lot of work, and it does. But the benefits are clear in that you will better understand the research materials *before* you start writing your paper. You will have read the materials; evaluated the sources; and used direct quotes from, paraphrased, or summarized the primary source material. Next you will start the actual writing of the first draft. The notecard method works best if you follow it completely; that is, for every reference you examine, you create a reference notecard, and for every idea you think you might want to use, you create an idea notecard. If you take the time to do this up front, it greatly facilitates creating the final product. You don't want to be scrambling for the journal title or volume number at the last minute when you are typing up your references, and if you used a reference notecard, you won't need to. You won't lose points for not providing the page number for a direct quote because the page number will be included on your idea notecard. Rearranging the reference notecards into alphabetical order will make typing your Reference section easy—you can do it straight from the notecards—and if your references are properly typed into Google Sheets, doing a "sort" to alphabetize them will be very easy. You can then just copy and paste to your Word document and double-check formatting requirements. Recording a single idea on an idea notecard will make it an easy task to organize, arrange, and rearrange ideas into a coherent story, complete with reference material and integrated in such a way as to demonstrate your scholarly writing ability. To this day, I still use my own variation of the notecard method because it leads to better synthesis of ideas and enhanced clarity.

ALTERNATE METHODS OF RECORDING AND USING RESEARCH NOTES

To be honest, my own variation of the notecard method involves using Microsoft Word, and I no longer physically write all the information on actual index cards. (Part of the reason is efficiency—my handwriting is awful!) There are a number of variations possible such as the Google Sheets version I discussed previously, but the essential ideas remain—carefully track your resource materials and deal with ideas one at a time. In this last section, I present some technology-based alternatives to using actual index cards.

Even though I like the old-school paper notecard method, there are disadvantages to it. There are now a number of computer-based alternatives available for use. Some of these techniques make use of general computer programs, and others are programs specifically designed for note-taking and writing. The advantages of taking notes using a computer program include the ability to (a) download from websites directly into a note file, (b) cut and paste data directly, (c) move information around electronically rather than physically, (d) have a legible set of notes no matter what your handwriting is like, and (e) cut and paste citation information directly. However, there are also disadvantages to computer note-taking: (a) You must have a digital device, likely web-enabled; (b) you must back up your notes after every session or else risk losing your work; (c) you must scroll to see your work, which makes it difficult to see the big picture; and (d) you must spend time moving information using cut and paste until your ideas are in the order you want, unless you become adept at using electronic annotation software. Computers crash, batteries die, internet signals are lost—sometimes bad things happen at the worst moments. There are also disadvantages to the paper version, such as interrupting your reading to take notes on index cards. In the end, you'll need to experiment with different approaches to see what works best for you.

You can use general software programs to customize your own computer-based note-taking approach. I use Microsoft Word to organize my references and my ideas and to integrate them into something I am writing. In my most recent research methods classes, I had students perform the notecard method using Google Sheets. However, I am one of those people who likes the tactile ability to move things around. Thus, after typing my idea notes into Word, I usually print them out and physically move them around until they are in an order I like, although I could do the same thing on a computer screen. There are specialized programs as well, such as Microsoft OneNote (Microsoft, n.d.), to assist in note-taking and information management. Some of the features of OneNote include the ability to capture webpages, create hyperlinks, insert file attachments, create tables, and use drawing tools; it can also recognize text embedded in pictures (Microsoft, n.d.). Using this program has the added benefit of direct integration with other Microsoft programs you may be using. Another software alternative is Nota Bene (Nota Bene, n.d.), which is designed for academic research and writing with word processing and database tools. Be sure to select an approach that meets your basic needs without being too complicated. Whichever approach you use, the ultimate goal is to be able to consider ideas individually and sort them while preserving the sources from which the ideas came. Using some variation of the notecard method in your scientific writing will help you tell a better story!

4

How to Write Your Psychology Paper With Style

General Tips

Well, then, I propose to you that, English Literature being (as we agreed) an Art, with a living and therefore improvable language for its medium or vehicle, a part—and no small part—of our business is to practise it. Yes, I seriously propose to you that here in Cambridge we practise writing: that we practise it not only for our own improvement, but to make, or at least try to make, appropriate, perspicuous, accurate, persuasive writing a recognisable hall-mark of anything turned out by our English School.

—SIR ARTHUR QUILLER-COUCH, *ON THE ART OF WRITING*

Now that you've gathered all your research notes and determined more or less how they will fit into your outline, I want to zoom out again and reexamine the guiding principles behind the writing endeavor on which you've embarked. These principles are what underpin scientific writing style, which we examine in this chapter. Why are you writing, aside from the fact that your instructor assigned you something to write? Ultimately, as a psychology student, you are writing to get a taste of what professional psychologists do, even if you never become an academic or professional psychologist. As stated in Chapter 1, psychologists continue threads of scientific discovery; however, to do this they have to communicate what they have discovered. They have to determine whether or not a particular paper will represent a true contribution to knowledge. Your instructors may not expect you to become a psychologist, but they attempt to model the intellectual demands and critical-thinking skills necessary to be a psychologist. So, how do you know whether your paper will contribute to the scientific knowledge base? Sternberg (2005) outlined eight ways to determine this:

1. The paper contains one or more surprising results that nevertheless make sense in some theoretical context. Whatever outcome occurs, you need to try to make sense of it, especially in the context of your study. For example, my research methods students often attempt to replicate a common finding

and fail to do so. The most common reason for this is that their study did not have enough participants.

2. The results presented in the paper are of major theoretical or practical significance. The best way for you to achieve this is to study an important topic. If you are studying an important topic, then the results may be important as well.

3. The ideas in the paper are new and exciting, perhaps presenting a new way of looking at an old problem. Students are often very good at achieving this because they can bring a fresh perspective to a problem or issue that psychologists tend to look at the same old way.

4. The interpretation of results is clear. This is where you get to apply the information you have learned from your statistics course. Using the appropriate descriptive and inferential statistics, you can draw conclusions about the problem being studied and have some certainty in your conclusion. Developing scientific, testable hypotheses allows the use of both quantitative and qualitative methods to interpret conclusions with clarity.

5. Your work integrates into a new, simpler framework data that had previously required a complex, possibly unwieldy framework. The ability to simplify complex relationships, when possible, is highly desirable in science, and this notion is sometimes referred to as *Occam's razor*. This is the idea that when two theories make the same prediction, the simpler theory is preferred to the more complex theory (Hiroshi, 1997). If your research can make this contribution, you have provided a highly valuable service to science.

6. The paper contains a major debunking of previously held ideas. To accomplish this goal, a good approach for students is to select a psychological myth or urban legend to test in their research study. Scientists are often drawn to counterintuitive findings (the opposite of what is expected), so if you can debunk a psychological myth or negate an urban legend, others will find value in your work.

7. The author presents an experiment with a particularly clever paradigm or experimental manipulation. If you can develop a new or innovative method of studying a complex phenomenon, the approach or methodology you use can almost be as valuable as the findings. Because psychology shares its secrets in the Method sections of journal articles, your contribution becomes public once you publish a journal article. Innovative ways of thinking about human behavior can lead to innovative approaches to studying that behavior in the laboratory or in the field.

8. The paper provides support for a theory based on the general findings. You can achieve this in your writing by not overreaching with your conclusions. From the storytelling perspective, this happens in Act III, where the climax occurs and the plot is resolved. Your research paper should end with broad statements that provide a general conclusion to what you have discovered through the course of your project.

Good scientists are good communicators. For their contribution to the scientific knowledge base to be accepted by other scientists, they must also use good storytelling techniques. That is, they make conscious choices about how to describe the main players in the story, the tone and approach, and the order in which they will narrate events. As mentioned in Chapter 1, the writer is not central to the scientific story; the topic is the main character, and in psychology, the topic is usually behavior. Objectivity is the hallmark of scientific writing, so the tone reflects distance from the topic, and the linear order of presentation reflects a thinking process that values measurable hypotheses and results above opinion. Of course, psychologists include opinions in their writing, but this is usually done in the form of shaping and presenting hypotheses, which are then dispassionately accepted or rejected.

Style, both in a general sense and American Psychological Association (APA) sense, actually simplifies some of the decision making that goes into scientific writing. Although the specifics of any particular writing assignment may differ, you will find that there are commonalities among types of scientific writing assignments in psychology. In this chapter, I present those common factors and how they may apply to particular writing assignments. Applying these general tips to all types of assignments is how you "practise writing," to borrow a phrase from the quote that begins this chapter.

WHY INSTRUCTORS LIKE TO READ STYLISH PAPERS

Instructors of undergraduate and graduate psychology instructors teach APA Style because it is our gold standard. Baker and Henrichsen (2002) said it better:

> In academic writing, the reader's response to a piece of writing is crucial. In a classroom situation the reader is also usually the teacher, and at least part of a paper's grade is generally based on how well it follows the accepted style. Proper formatting is the hallmark of a detail-oriented researcher. A writer who makes stylesheet errors because he or she believes they are "no big deal" might be surprised when evaluators question other details of the paper, such as the data on which the conclusions are based. After all—if a writer can't get all the periods in the right places, how can he or she be expected to correctly calculate an ANOVA or t-test? (para. 3)

The *Publication Manual* (APA, 2020) actually serves multiple functions: It is a style manual—it addresses sentence structure issues, grammar, how to compose paragraphs, and so forth—and it is also a presentation guide—it addresses how the manuscript should appear in print and electronic format. For the sake of clarity, I refer to *APA Style* as the mode of expression and *APA format* as the mode of presentation. Both topics are covered in detail in this book: APA formatting issues are addressed in this chapter; in Chapters 5 and 6 on literature reviews and research papers, respectively, issues of both APA Style and APA formatting are further explored.

Just how important is it to prepare a manuscript using APA Style and format? Obviously, the answer will vary depending on the instructor and the assignment. Remember, though, that the *Publication Manual* was originally created for psychologists wanting to publish their work in scholarly journals. The editor of a journal is the person ultimately responsible for deciding what gets published and what does not. Do journal editors really care about APA Style and format, or is it just a formality? Brewer et al. (2001) asked that question to hundreds of psychology journal editors, and the results are interesting. As it turns out, to some journal editors APA format is extremely important: "39% of the respondents reported that they *had* returned a manuscript to an author purely for failing to adhere to APA Style" (p. 266). When asked about the most common problems, the journal editors listed the top three problem areas as references, tables and figures, and mathematics and statistics. This subset of editors who desired strict adherence to APA Style were labeled "APA Style sticklers" (Brewer et al., 2001, p. 267).

Many types of scientific writing in psychology share components of the same overall style. In later chapters, I address very specific details about assignments and their particular requirements, but it is useful to review here the general style used for most scientific writing. Exhibit 4.1 provides a quick overview of the general sections you may be asked to write.

The ability to write clearly and concisely is an essential skill in becoming a good scientist. Throughout this book, I emphasize the importance of clarity and the ability to tell a coherent story. Psychologists follow the *Publication Manual* as a general guide, and it provides detailed information about the style that scientific writing should follow and the format in which it should appear. Many psychology departments require that student papers, theses, and dissertations be prepared according to the *Publication Manual*. Of course when departmental requirements differ from those in the *Publication Manual,* the departmental or institutional requirements take precedence. At its essence, the *Publication Manual* is the instruction guide to authors on how to communicate psychological findings to the scientific community.

In this chapter, I highlight some of the most common areas of concern for writing in APA Style and format. Obviously, the *Publication Manual* is the comprehensive source that addresses almost every possible nuance of a research-paper-writing situation you may face. I am selective in what to address here; I want you to be prepared for the most common situations, and for the rare events, consulting the *Publication Manual* will be a good idea. For instance, the rules for preparing a figure in APA format are very precise (in fact, there are entire books about preparing tables and figures in APA format). Fortunately, figures are often not necessary for undergraduate writing projects.

Manuscript Preparation

One of the most important points to remember when submitting work for any college class is that it is a representation of the quality of your skills and abilities. Every time you hand in an assignment, make sure it is your very best work. If you are submitting a rough draft of a section of your research paper, and the

Exhibit 4.1. Typical Sections of an APA Style Research Paper

Title page (take credit, provide details)

    Title (boldfaced, centered, in upper half of title page)

    Author's name (as it matches course records)

    Author's department or program, followed by author's affiliation

    Course number, course name

    Instructor's name

    Due date

    Page number (inside top one-inch margin)

Abstract (quick comprehensive summary)

    Typically not longer than 250 words

    Keywords provide searchable terms for paper

    Some assignments, no abstract required

Introduction (what topic you are studying)

    Introduce the research problem (or thesis statement)

    Develop the background, identify gap in literature

    State the purpose and rationale for the paper, state hypotheses

Method (what steps are followed)

    Participants, materials, and procedure.

    Should be in enough detail to replicate work if desired.

Results (what are the outcomes, statistically speaking)

    Hypotheses: Supported or refuted?

    Presentation of statistical outcomes: tables, figures as necessary

    Presentation, not interpretation

Discussion (what it all means, what should happen next)

    Was the gap filled/mystery solved?

    Outcomes make sense?

    Are these outcomes really meaningful?

    What are the avenues for future research?

Reference section (give credit where credit is due)

    All items cited in paper are presented here

    APA *PM* 7e reference style followed

    Not a bibliography; only present items here cited in text

ink smudges on any of the pages, reprint that page. If the dog started eating your homework, redo or recopy that page. When you hand in work that has a sloppy appearance, some professors may jump to the conclusion that your thinking is also sloppy. You would never dream of sending a resume to a prospective employer that had typographical errors or obvious formatting blunders in it—why would you do so for your instructors? Be sure to follow these rules for manuscript preparation in APA format, but also be sure to heed any formatting exceptions that the instructor gives you.

Word Processing: Typing and Layout

With regard to page layout, here are the requirements for APA format:

- The fonts recommended in the seventh edition of the *Publication Manual* are Calibri 11-point, Arial 11-point, Lucida Sans Unicode 10-point, Times New Roman 12-point, Georgia 11-point, and Computer Modern 10-point. Whichever you choose, use the same font throughout the entire paper. Check with your instructor to see if they have a preference or requirement.

- Double-space everything, but you can use single- or double-spacing in tables and figures.

- Set 1-in. margins at the top, bottom, left, and right of the page.

- Start the following sections on a new page: title page, abstract, Introduction, references, appendices, tables, figures, and figure captions.

- Number every page. Use the automatic page number function in your word-processing program to generate page numbers in your file.

- Indent each paragraph 1/2 in. (this is usually the default setting).

- Use one space after commas, colons, semicolons, periods in the reference section, and periods in the initials of a person's name. Use one space after end-of-sentence punctuation, unless your instructor indicates otherwise.

Headings and Series

Headings are used to help organize the flow of the text and give readers signposts for where they are in the manuscript. In the sample paper at the end of Chapter 7, you will see the typical three heading levels used in APA papers. (The *Publication Manual* includes one to five levels of heading.) The headings are differentiated by capital or lowercase letters, boldface, italics, centered text, and so forth.

Seriation refers to the presentation of multiple items within a sentence, for example, whether you are providing a step-by-step sequence (1-2-3) or just listing different items (a-b-c). The rules for seriation are straightforward: When the individual items within a series do not contain a comma, use commas to separate them (e.g., "The key items to remember are (a) be honest, (b) be brave, and (c) be true"). If the individual items within a series do contain a comma, use semicolons to separate them (e.g., "To pilot test the new instrument, we (a) generated a list of potential items, based on participant interviews; (b) developed potential survey items, using a Likert-type scale; and (c) completed the survey with volunteers from a college course in psychometrics").

Abbreviations and Numbers

Like many scientists, psychologists tend to use jargon specific to the discipline. Often, jargon is expressed in the form of abbreviations. The *Publication Manual* advises using abbreviations sparingly. There are places where repeating a particular phrase (e.g., "cumulative final exam score") is cumbersome and using an abbreviation makes sense (e.g., CFES). However, my advice is to only use an abbreviation if it makes it easier for the reader (not the writer). Be careful in assuming that an abbreviation is so common that all readers will know what it means. In general, spell out an abbreviation the first time it is used, with the abbreviation in parentheses afterward. Then you can use the abbreviation (without parentheses) throughout the remainder of your paper. Be sure to use the appropriate scientific abbreviations in text; the *Publication Manual* lists these. If you choose to use Latin abbreviations, remember that they are not italicized. Table 4.1 contains helpful Latin abbreviations and their meanings.

To be honest, the use of numbers in an APA-formatted paper is confusing. There are general rules, but there appear to be as many exceptions as there are rules. Generally, numbers below 10 are spelled out as words (zero, one, two, three, four, etc.) and numbers 10 and above are expressed as numerals (10, 11, 12, 13, etc.). The under-10 rule, however, does not apply to numbers that represent time, dates, ages, scores and points on a scale, exact sums of money, and numerals as numerals. Also remember that if you start a sentence with a number, you must spell out the number in words and use proper capitalization (e.g., "Thirty-two general psychology students completed the survey"). In general,

TABLE 4.1. Latin Abbreviations

Abbreviation	What it means	Sample sentence
cf.	compare	APA Style and format based on the *Publication Manual* are designed to provide scientific notation to researcher's ideas (cf. expression of ideas with the *Chicago Manual of Style*).
e.g.	for example	There are different types of doctoral degrees in psychology (e.g., PhD, PsyD, EdD).
etc.	and so forth	There are numerous variables that influence a student's decision to attend college (such as school prestige, amount of financial aid, distance from home, availability of a major, etc.).
i.e.	that is	There is not much evidence that seat time (i.e., time on task) is directly related to student performance in the classroom.
viz.	namely	Although there are multiple organizations for psychologists to become involved in, as is the case in other sciences, often the largest organization possesses the greatest degree of political clout (viz., the American Psychological Association).
vs.	versus	Developmental psychologists will probably never completely understand the contributions of heredity and environment (i.e., the nature vs. nurture debate).
et al.	and others	These three authors (Smith et al., 2020) concluded that the impact on low birthweight was greater for children of low-income families as compared with children of high-income families.

avoid starting a sentence with a number. APA format dictates that numerical measurement be expressed in metric units—centimeters and meters rather than inches and feet. For the more explicit rules concerning the use of numbers, see the *Publication Manual*.

Citations and Quotations in Text

Good scientific writing places an idea about a variable or behavior in context. That is, part of the story is the backstory that contributes to our current state of knowledge about a phenomenon and, in a research paper, the gap or hole in the knowledge that the research paper strives to fill. To accomplish this goal, however, you must be familiar with the existing literature, which is why you conduct library research on your topic, extract materials, and synthesize those materials into coherent paragraphs. An essential component of this task is the ability to cite the work of others in your own work—in other words, giving credit where credit is due. The inability to give credit would be an instance of plagiarism.

As a psychology student, you are already accustomed to this practice in science. In books and articles, even your introductory psychology textbook, you can see examples where the flowing text is interrupted by last names and a year, sometimes in parentheses, sometimes not in parentheses. This practice, called *citation* or *citing,* is vital to scientific writing. We cannot borrow others' ideas without proper attribution. The ability to cite (using proper APA format of course) is one way to show that you are developing into a scholar. Students sometimes worry that an introduction or a literature review is not very original because it is filled with the citations of others' work. However, the originality comes from how you put those ideas together; your unique contribution is the thread or synthesis or common theme you identified and then documented with your citations. The ability to identify common themes where they exist is a highly valuable intellectual skill; therefore, using proper citation methods (and reference lists) helps you demonstrate your abilities as a psychological scientist.

In APA format there are basically three ways to present citations in the text of your paper: author name(s) and publication year outside of parentheses; author name(s) outside of parentheses, publication year in parentheses; and author name(s) and publication year inside parentheses.

- It was in 1956 that G. A. Miller published his famous article about memory and information processing regarding seven plus or minus two.

- In his famous article, G. A. Miller (1956) presented the ideas about memory and information processing in the form of seven plus or minus two.

- In a famous article long ago the classic ideas were presented about memory and information processing in the form of seven plus or minus two (G. A. Miller, 1956).

How do you decide which format to use? Consider the overall flow of the paragraph and make a selection that avoids the passive voice. See Table 4.2 for sample sentences using the variety of forms.

TABLE 4.2. Examples of Citation Styles With Varying Numbers of Authors

No. of citations or authors	Author and publication year outside of parentheses	Author outside parentheses, publication year inside parentheses	Both author and publication year inside parentheses
One citation, one author only	Updated suggestions for how to launch a course via the first day of class were offered by Robinson in 2019.	Engaging students on the first day of class is critical to setting positive course expectations, according to Robinson (2019).	Student-generated questions can be effectively used to set the tone of the course beginning from the very first day (Robinson, 2019).
One citation, more than one author	It's important to know what type of situation provides the best research training for undergraduates; fortunately, in 2019 Burke and Prieto addressed this issue.	According to Burke and Prieto (2019), the higher quality the research training environment, the higher the student reported ratings of research self-efficacy.	It appears that after careful study, high quality research training environments are as important for undergraduate students as they are for graduate students (Burke & Prieto, 2019).

There may be cases when you need to reference two or more citations in the same sentence. This is usually accomplished inside parentheses. You separate the references with semicolons, and order them alphabetically by the first author's last name, not by year of publication. Note that outside of parentheses, you use "and" between authors' names (or, with three or more authors, start with the first author's last name and et al. from the first citation onward); however, inside parentheses, you use an ampersand (&) between authors' names.

As you can imagine, there are also detailed rules for the presentation of quotations in text. Follow the citation styles noted previously; however, in addition you must include the page number on which (or paragraph in which) the quotation appeared (this is why, using the notecard method, you should write down the page number of any passage that you think you might use as a direct quote). Overall, be sure to follow the instructor's preferences for the use of direct quotes in your research paper assignment. As I've alluded to earlier, I am not a fan of multiple direct quotes in research papers—they should be used only when the original author has said something so perfectly that paraphrasing it would not communicate the same thought. I think students sometimes see direct quotes as a way to have to write less, and I often tell my students that a string of direct quotes does not make a scholarly paper. You exhibit your research talent much more clearly when you take a complicated passage and paraphrase it into simpler terms. If you are going to use direct quotes, be sure to follow the rules of APA format.

If you plan to use a quote of 40 words or more, you must use a block format in text to set off the quote. If you omit part of a quote, you must note that by using ellipsis marks (. . .) within the quote; however, be sure that your deletion does not change the meaning of the original idea. Remember that you cannot use ellipses at the beginning or end of a direct quote. If you want to add emphasis to the original quote (e.g., by italicizing a word), you must acknowledge that you added the italics to the text (i.e., that what you have italicized was not in italics in the original quote). If you are quoting from a source with page numbers, you must include a page number (e.g., "p. 278"). If you are reporting from a source without page numbers (e.g., a brochure or a website), you must cite the paragraph number using the paragraph symbol (e.g., "para. 7") or you need to provide some sort of description to allow the reader to locate the source material you used.

Tables and Figures

There is extensive coverage of table and figure presentation in the *Publication Manual*—in fact, 24 table examples and 21 figure examples are included in the seventh edition. Tables are fairly common in research papers because they can present a large volume of information in an efficient amount of space. Even though tables are efficient, don't over-rely on them; you only want to use a table if it is integral to the story. Don't use a table just to say you used a table (unless a table is part of a research paper assignment). Tables need to be explicitly mentioned in your text; often that's in the Method or Results section (e.g., "See Table 1 for the means and standard deviations for the survey items"). Tables are single- or double-spaced and cannot contain vertical rules to separate columns. Table titles are italicized. For more details on table preparation, refer to the *Publication Manual*. I also present more information on tables in Chapter 7.

Figures are used in a research paper to present graphical or pictorial information. In the appropriate context, figures can be invaluable for telling a complex story, but figure preparation is also complex. Not only are there precise rules for figure preparation, but in APA format a figure also requires a figure caption to explain the figure. The sample sections and complete sample paper in Chapter 7 present a typical table, but not a figure. For more explicit details on figure preparation, see the *Publication Manual*.

AUDIENCE APPROVAL METER: ASK WHAT YOU ARE BEING GRADED ON

Essentially, the advice I have given you about "giving the instructor the assignment the way they want it" also applies when I submit manuscripts for publication in journals. We all have to follow the professional expectations of the discipline when making our work public. At times, this is frustrating because different faculty members (and different journals) may use slightly different criteria in deciding whether a research paper is good or if a manuscript is publishable. The strategy to follow is to find out as much as possible about the evaluation standards of whomever will be reviewing your work. Ideally, with your scientific writing assignments, an instructor may be able to provide a grading rubric before you submit your written work. This rubric will give you an idea of your instructor's expectations and what the point values are for particular parts of an assignment. Figure 4.1 is a sample rubric I use when grading an introduction section for my undergraduate, upper division research methods course.

FIGURE 4.1. Sample Rubric for Grading an Introduction Section (continues)

PSYC 321 Research Methods
Spring 2019

Rubric Details for Introduction Section Assignment

Completion of Assignment (25 points)

- Introduce the reader to the issue in the first paragraph. Convince the reader that this is an important issue. Perhaps it impacts a large number of people, or it is an essential component of daily life. Try to impress upon the reader the importance of the issue. Using some general statistics (with citations) here.
- Review the available literature on the topic. If there are studies related specifically to your topic, review them here. If there are no specific studies, then broaden your review of the literature to include related areas. Show that you have done your scholarly homework. You are providing a context for your study. There should be multiple studies cited in this section of your introduction. Start this subsection broad and end narrow.
- Within this context, identify a problem or area where the knowledge is incomplete. This turns into your statement of the problem to be addressed by this research. You have reviewed the literature, but there is a gap in the literature—an unresolved problem or issue. The goal of your study is to fill that gap by conducting your study. Provide a clear statement of purpose for the current study. In fact, conclude this subsection with a sentence that starts with "**The purpose of my study is to....**"
- Then, give a brief overview of the methodology that will be used to address the knowledge gap. Just a snapshot of the participants, materials, and basic procedure used in the study. This is a preview – "coming attractions."
- Conclude your Introduction section with specific hypotheses to be tested or expected outcomes. What do you expect to happen? Develop your working hypotheses based on your expectations and your review of the literature. The more specific you are here, the easier it will be to write survey questions, and the easier it will be to select the appropriate statistical analyses later. Your hypotheses might examine differences between certain groups, associations or relationships between variables, etc. Start each hypothesis sentence with "**I hypothesize that....**"

Clarity of Presentation, Including Mechanics and Grammar (40 points)

- Spelling, grammar, punctuation, noun-verb agreement all correctly followed; obvious mistakes avoided (paper was proofread).
- Avoid direct quotations, but if used, a maximum of three; a scholarly paper is not a string of direct quotations.
- Use of verb tense and noun and pronoun number should be correct and consistent.
- Use of personal pronouns is non-sexist.
- When discussing individuals with disabilities, put the person first (i.e., "a student with anorexia" is preferred over "an anorexic student."
- Transitions between sections should be smooth, and you should avoid awkward sentence constructions.
- Write in complete sentences. Each paragraph focuses on a single topic.
- Avoid being colloquial (informal) in your writing. Be formal, and do not write like you are having a conversation.
- No contractions (e.g., didn't, can't, wouldn't, shouldn't).

FIGURE 4.1. Sample Rubric for Grading an Introduction Section (continued)

- No abbreviations unless APA-approved.
- Avoid passive voice.
- Do not use 'we' or 'us'– this is a single author paper from the first person perspective.
- Avoid overzealous claims, such as correlations data being interpreted as causal, or using the word "prove."
- No anthropomorphizing/avoid the pathetic fallacy error: avoid "data indicate," "research found."
- Be specific and precise – avoid using the word "thing."

Proper Use of APA Style and Formatting (35 points)

APA Writing Style	Microsoft Word Formatting
• Evidence is cited using a paraphrase of the author's ideas (with proper citation), or direct quote (with proper citation and page or paragraph number). • Acronyms are defined prior to the first use of the acronym. • Claims made by the author are supported with evidence (citations); give credit where credit is due to avoid plagiarism. • There are specific rules for the display of numbers/numerals in APA style; be sure to follow those rules and note the exceptions to the rules. • Use "and" and "&" properly with in-text citations. • Use et al. for reference citations following APA rules. • Punctuation should be placed inside quotation marks (either single or double quotation marks). • Repeat the title of paper at the top of the Introduction section on page 3.	• One-inch margin on all four sides of the page. • Entire paper is double-spaced, with no extra spaces between paragraphs or manuscript sections. • Page number inside the top 1-inch margin. • No right justification of text (should be ragged right margin). • Use same font throughout; select from APA-approved list • If a block quote is used (40 words or more), it is properly indented. • If headings/subheadings are used, they must be properly formatted. • If a list is included, use proper APA rules for seriation.

TELLING AND RETELLING YOUR STORY: DRAFTING, EDITING, REVISING, AND PROOFREADING

As you begin drafting your paper, you should also be working on your reference list at the same time. If you are using the notecard method or some form of it, you are already doing that work. The *Publication Manual* is very specific in its rules, but the overriding principle for a reference citation is to provide the reader with enough bibliographic information to find the reference. It should act as a guide to where you extracted the information. The four fundamental parts of a reference citation include the authorship, the date published, the title of the work, and how the work can be located (APA, 2020). A complete reference citation is important because it allows any reader to retrace the "intellectual journey" that brought you to your conclusions.

Writing the Rough Draft

If you have been following my advice from previous chapters, writing your first rough draft will not be so daunting. You have a research question or thesis statement, and you have done a review of the literature and gathered your research articles. You have read everything carefully while recording your reference notecards and idea notecards, and now you are ready to write. Because you have placed one idea on each card, you can easily arrange and rearrange your ideas into paragraphs. But, even with all the wonderful background work you have done, it's time to start writing.

As with any important project, sometimes it's hard to get started. Writers (not just student writers) often want the words to come out perfectly the first time around. Although that might be nice, it rarely happens. The overall goal of a rough draft is to get you started, and then later in the process you can edit, revise, and proofread. Being perfectionistic in your expectations of your first draft may cause you to procrastinate. A little procrastination is okay, but too much will lead to panic and cramming at the last minute, and may not allow you to do your best work. Some helpful suggestions for writing your rough draft follow.

To help avoid procrastination, allow yourself to write an imperfect rough draft. I often tell my students that it is much easier to edit than to create. However, before you can edit, you first have to generate some content. Staring at a blank page or a blank computer screen can be intimidating—the best cure is to start writing.

You know yourself better than anyone. It may be unreasonable for you to block out time on Saturday from 1:00 p.m. to 7:00 p.m. You know your best times of day; try to do some of your writing during those windows. Waiting until 1:00 a.m., when you finally have some time, is also not a good idea. Write in short spurts—promise yourself that you will write nonstop for 15 to 30 minutes, without any distractions. If you string together enough of these 15- to 30-minute writing sessions, eventually you'll have a rough draft. And if you start your assignment early enough, you won't need to panic and try to complete everything minutes before it is due.

It's okay to take breaks. Get up from your computer and stretch. Use Pomodoro (a time management technique). Get something to drink. But don't make the breaks longer than the writing session. If your mind (or heart) isn't into writing, then do something else. But at those times when you are in the mood to write, write! I have to tell you that I'm this way; if I'm not in the mood to write, then I don't do it—I go do something else. But when my brain is in that "writing mode," I try to milk it for all it's worth and get as much done as I can. Before you take a break, try to map out what you will be writing about next time you sit down to write. Leave yourself some notes, or a skeleton outline in your file, so that when you come back to it you'll be able to jump-start yourself and pick up your thoughts.

Save all of your rough drafts and all of your notes about your paper. As you go through the editing and revising process, you may cut out sentences or even paragraphs, then realize later on that you want to put something back in. If you do all your writing and editing in one file, deleted information is likely to be gone (unless you are using Microsoft Word's "Track Changes" mode, in which case writing a rough draft would be cumbersome). So name your first rough draft, for example, "term paper draft 1.0," then whenever you make minor revisions, use the "Save As" function and rename the next file "draft 1.1," "draft 1.2," and so forth. Whenever I complete a major revision, I bump the revision number up to "draft 2.0," and so on. This will leave you with a trail of your rough drafts, which is also a nice way to demonstrate the work that you did throughout the writing process.

Editing Your Work

Editing can occur at multiple times in the writing process. However, editing cannot occur until there is something to edit! Thus, getting anything down for a rough draft, no matter how rough it is, allows you to begin the process of improvement. Many authors recommend valuable tips for the editing process, such as placing a ruler under each line as you read it so that your eyes have a manageable amount of text to review (University of Arkansas at Little Rock, n.d.). Here are some helpful suggestions and tips for editing from Texas A&M University (n.d.):

- After you finish your rough draft, set it aside for a period of time before looking at it again. This will allow you to review it with a fresh perspective.

- If you are going to self-edit, double or triple space your draft so you'll have room to write down suggestions.

- Be brutal with yourself; don't settle, and don't take shortcuts. Delete, substitute, rearrange, insert, and create new if you need to.

- Give special consideration to beginning and ending paragraphs.

- Read it out loud. You will hear some mistakes that you didn't see. Just take care to read each word verbatim—our brains autocorrect many of the errors that can occur. Better yet, have someone else read your draft out loud to you.

- Keep a list of your most common errors so that you can improve and learn to avoid those errors in the future.

  More editing suggestions are offered by Lipkewich (2001):

- Read your own work backwards. Read the last sentence, then the second-to-last sentence, and so on.

- Does each sentence make sense when you read it on its own?

- Do you see or hear any errors in the sentence?

- Be sure that every sentence has two parts: the subject (who or what) and the predicate (what is happening).

- Use sentence-combining words such as "and," "but," "or," "yet," "who," "whom," "which," "that," "whose," "because," "although," "when," "if," and "where."

- Use periods and commas where necessary, but do not overuse them.

- Do not overuse the exclamation point.

- Use a dictionary to check spelling in addition to any software spell-checkers you may use.

Revising Your Work

You've completed the hard work of creating the best rough draft that you can, and you have sought out editorial comment. You may have self-edited, had a peer edit your work, or perhaps your instructor edited and/or graded your rough draft. Your draft may have been returned to you with tracked changes and comments in the file. With this invaluable feedback, now it's time to revise your work.

Revising is simply looking back at your writing and making changes. What types of changes? You might decide to add new information that you can now see is missing, or you might take out information you now know is unnecessary or tangential to your main topic. You might rearrange the order or sequence of ideas, sentences, or even complete paragraphs to tell a more compelling story, and you might change or substitute words now that you can begin to see the big picture coming together. Revising is *not* proofreading for typographical errors or misplaced words, and just because you used spell-check does not mean that the revision process is complete (Empire State College, n.d.). Consider the first draft of a simulated student paper (Figure 4.2). I've created this so it would be a realistic first draft of part of a term paper or literature review that a student might be working on.

Remember, the goal of a first draft is to just get ideas down. Rather than marking every spelling mistake and instance of incorrect citation style, your instructor may instead give you a list of broader goals for improving your work, expecting you to make the finer corrections yourself. If I were grading this sample paper, I might create a list of revision feedback that included the following:

- Focus your first paragraph a little better. First, get rid of the word "thing" because it's too vague. Second, I think readers will agree that hate and hate crimes are painful, so expand on the ways in which hate is real. I'm not sure I get the connection between fast-paced lifestyles, stress, and hate. Anger, yes, but why hate?

- OK, I see what you mean about societal changes leading to hate. Interesting idea that without a stratified class system, we create our own in- and out-groups. What does "introversion" mean?

- Please clarify: Do you think discrimination is the most significant domestic social issue of our times *because* it has caused the most violence? Is this the way Newman defined its significance? Your citations are not in APA Style—please correct.

- Need smoother transition between second and third paragraph. "Newman points out a problem. . . ." Huh? Sounds like you are about to move to a new topic.

- Not clear where Whillock quote begins and ends. Who's cited at end of paragraph 3?

- Link the sentence about Salem witch hunts, and relevance of these examples to the idea that defining values goes hand in hand with defining what is not valued.

- Please proofread. There are a few obvious spelling mistakes.

FIGURE 4.2. Sample Paper on Hate, Rough Draft

Hate is a very real and painful thing in our society today. We have seen case after case all throughout history where hate crimes have been committed mainly towards groups of minorities. Today's lifestyle is fast paced, stressful and the society has changed. These factors combined cause flared anger and frustrations. These things lead us to the hate that we see displayed today.

In a society that has fundamentally rejected class and caste, each of us looks elsewhere for identifications. The result has been a tendency toward introversions and "in-group" association, the manifestations of which are too often bigotry, prejudice and discrimination against those thought to constitute the "out-group." Tacitly accepted for so long as imply a fact of American life discrimination has now emerged as probably the most significant domestic social issue of our times, and already quite the most violent (Newman 1-2).

Newman points out a problem our society has today. This is a problem that has been created by the society itself, and it is a problem that needs to be handled in a sociological manner. Whillock argues that "hate is not viewed as outside the bounds of societal interest. From societal sanctioning of the Salem witch-hunts or the McCrthy hearings, to outrage over Wounded Knee and Mi Lai, American history is replete with examples of how society has attempted to come to terms with acts of hatred. Such struggles will continue to exist as longs as we keep trying to define (or redefine) our culture's values and the consequent objects for its disdain (47).

When you look at the final draft (Figure 4.3), you'll notice that the student took charge of the line edits and proofreading and took some of the suggestions but ignored others. This is typically OK unless you are ignoring a key point that your instructor has been emphasizing. The text becomes a bit shorter, but it reads much better. You may have to go through more than one revision cycle; also, try to have as many people look at it as possible. Have a classmate review your work (and offer to review theirs). Ask your instructor (if possible) or a teaching assistant to review your work so you have multiple revision opportunities. And remember, you will only have time for this revision process if you finish your drafts ahead of time—the last-minute approach does not allow for revisions and improvements.

FIGURE 4.3. Sample Paper on Hate, Revised

Hate is a real phenomenon in society today. We see case after case throughout history where hate crimes were committed toward groups of minorities. Today's lifestyle is fast paced and stressful, and the society has changed. These complexities combined cause anger, frustration, and the hate we see displayed today.

In a society that has fundamentally rejected class and caste, each of us looks elsewhere for identifications. The result is a tendency toward introversions and "in-group" association, the manifestations of which are bigotry, prejudice, and discrimination. Tacitly accepted for so long as simply a fact of American life, discrimination is now probably the most significant domestic social issue of our time, and it is already quite violent (Newman, 2002).

Newman (2002) stated that this problem was created by society, and it is a problem that needs to be addressed from a sociological perspective. Whillock (2003) argued that "hate is not viewed as outside the bounds of societal interest" (p. 492). From societal sanctioning of the Salem witch hunts or the McCarthy hearings, to outrage over Wounded Knee and Mi Lai, American history is replete with examples of how society has attempted to come to terms with acts of hatred. Such struggles will continue to exist as long as society strives to define (or redefine) our culture's core values and future objects of disdain (Newman, 2002).

This revision process is common throughout all of scientific writing. In fact, your faculty members who do research and publish know much about revision. Rarely, and I mean rarely, will a scholarly paper be accepted on its first submission to a professional journal. In fact, the outcome that most aspiring scientists hope for is "revise and resubmit," sometimes called "R & R." That is, the journal has technically rejected the first submission for publication, but the editorial feedback is for the author to revise his or her work and resubmit it, hoping for an eventual acceptance. The process that faculty members follow with their students, draft–edit–revise, is the exact process that faculty members follow in their professional careers. One of the reasons faculty members invest so much time and effort into grading and marking student papers is because we are modeling the professional practices of our discipline for students.

Proofreading Your Work

The last stage in this draft–edit–revise cycle is proofreading. When you think you are about done with your final product, proofreading is the process of making final corrections and changes to your near-finished paper. What types of errors are you looking for at this stage of the process? According to Hibbard (n.d.), the most common errors identified during proofreading are incorrectly spelled names, reversed numbers, incorrect dates, incorrect or inconsistent capitalization, duplicate words or phrases, omission of words or parts of words, incorrect or missing punctuation, nonagreement of subject and verb, and misspelled words. Proofreading is not the stage for creating new sections of the paper, or making major changes—that should have been accomplished during the revision process. Proofreading is the "fine tuning" that occurs before that wonderful feeling of being finished with a quality product.

Numerous authors have offered advice to facilitate successful proofreading. Taking the suggestions of Hibbard (n.d.), the University of Arkansas at Little Rock (n.d.), and the University of North Carolina at Chapel Hill (n.d.), I created the checklist in Exhibit 4.2 as a guide to proofreading.

Finally, as suggested previously regarding the rough draft process, read every word out loud or have someone else read every word out loud to you. This will help you identify missing or extra words (Szuchman, 2005).

HOW TO AVOID PLAGIARISM WITH STYLE AND GOOD ACADEMIC CITIZENSHIP

What is plagiarism? According to Landau (n.d., para. 3), "Plagiarism occurs when people take credit for thoughts, words, images, musical passages, or ideas originally created by someone else." The Council of Writing Program Administrators (2003, para. 4) defined plagiarism as "when a writer deliberately uses someone else's language, ideas, or other original (not common-knowledge) material without acknowledging its source." Essentially, plagiarism is the failure

EXHIBIT 4.2. Proofreading Checklist

Check (√) one

Yes	No	Proofreading Questions to Consider
____	____	Did you proofread from a printed copy (not from the computer screen)?
____	____	Did you look for words that are commonly misused? (A list of these is presented in Exhibit 4.5.)
____	____	Did you allow some time to pass between finishing the last revision and your final proofreading?
____	____	Did you proofread one last time before you printed or sent the final copy?
____	____	Are there matching open and closed quotation marks and parentheses?
____	____	Is the punctuation spaced consistently?
____	____	Is there too much or too little space anywhere in the final draft?
____	____	Have all the names and dates been checked and double checked?
____	____	Are all the bullets aligned?
____	____	Are all the word divisions (hyphenations) correct?
____	____	Have you used spell-check and grammar-check?
____	____	Did you proofread for one type of error at a time?
____	____	Did you read slowly and read every word?
____	____	Did you check to make sure there were no changes in font type or font size throughout the work?
____	____	If you prepared your work in Mac Pages or Google Docs and converted it to Microsoft Word to hand in, did you check the converted Microsoft Word document to see if APA formatting was properly preserved?
____	____	If you are uploading your file to a learning management system and if the instructor has rules for file names, did you follow the precise rules for file names?
____	____	Did you review the rubric and make sure all parts of your work comply with the instructor's expectations?
____	____	Did you ensure every sentence ends with a punctuation mark?
____	____	Are you satisfied with your work?

to give credit where credit is due. There are serious consequences for students who are caught plagiarizing; these vary from instructor to instructor as well as from institution to institution. You should be able to find detailed information about this in your institution's student handbook. The consequences could be receiving an F on the assignment, an F in the course, and, in some cases, academic probation and/or loss of scholarships.

Harris (2005) and Landau (n.d.) suggested two main types of plagiarism—intentional and unintentional. Intentional plagiarism is a purposeful act in which deception on the part of the writer is premeditated. Exhibit 4.3 presents examples of what most would consider acts of intentional plagiarism. Unintentional plagiarism occurs when there is no intent to plagiarize, yet it happens anyway. This may be from a lack of knowledge about proper citation

---

EXHIBIT 4.3. Examples of Intentional Plagiarism

- Downloading and turning in a paper from the internet, including a webpage or paper mill essay
- Copying and pasting phrases, sentences, or paragraphs into your paper without showing a quotation or adding the proper citation
- Paraphrasing or summarizing a source's words or ideas without proper citation
- Including a graph, table, or picture from a source without proper citation
- Getting so much help from a tutor or writing helper that the paper or part of the paper is no longer honestly your work
- Turning in previously written work when that practice is prohibited by your instructor
- Taking someone else's ideas and claiming them to be your own original ideas

---

Note. From *Using Sources Effectively: Strengthening Your Writing and Avoiding Plagiarism* (2nd ed., p. 14), by R. A. Harris, 2005. Copyright 2005 by Pyrczak. Reprinted with permission.

rules, carelessness, inappropriate use of a source, or other inadvertent actions (Council of Writing Program Administrators, 2003; Harris, 2005).

Sometimes it is difficult to differentiate between plagiarism and sloppy citation style, which emphasizes the importance of your instructors teaching you about proper citations (in our case, APA Style) and how to avoid plagiarism. Let me present you with some of these "sticky situations" and practice a bit to determine whether the writing constitutes plagiarism or the misuse of sources. The idea for this exercise comes from Shadle (2006). Here is the original text from Price (2002), followed by the source in proper APA reference format:

> But plagiarism is not stable. What we think of as plagiarism shifts across historical time periods, across cultures, across workplaces, even across academic disciplines. We need to stop treating plagiarism like a pure moral absolute ("Thou shalt not plagiarize") and start explaining it in a way that accounts for these shifting features of contexts.

> Price, M. (2002). Beyond "gotcha!": Situating plagiarism in policy and pedagogy. *College Composition and Communication, 54*(1), 88–115. https://doi.org/10.2307/1512103

If you were going to use that as a direct quote in your paper, here is what it would look like (note that the text is indented because the quote is longer than 40 words):

> But plagiarism is not stable. What we think of as plagiarism shifts across historical time periods, across cultures, across workplaces, even across academic disciplines. We need to stop treating plagiarism like a pure moral absolute ("Thou shalt not plagiarize") and start explaining it in a way that accounts for these shifting features of contexts. (Price, 2002, p. 90)

But what if a student were to write the following—would this be plagiarism?

> Plagiarism is very difficult to understand because it is not stable. What we think of as plagiarism shifts across historical time periods, across cultures, across workplaces, even across academic disciplines. We need to stop treating plagiarism like a pure moral absolute and start explaining it in a way that accounts for these shifting features of contexts.

For most faculty, the answer would be yes, this is plagiarism. Not only are most of the phrases identical to the original, but there is absolutely no attribution to the author (remember, we must give credit where credit is due). If I were to read a paragraph like this in a student's paper, I would have to assume that this idea was the student's original idea because of the lack of attribution.

The previous example is fairly blatant, but what about this one?

> According to Price, plagiarism is not stable. What we think of as plagiarism shifts across historical time periods, across cultures, across workplaces, even across academic disciplines. We need to stop treating plagiarism like a pure moral absolute and start explaining it in a way that accounts for these shifting features of contexts (90).

I would consider this example either unintentional plagiarism or sloppy citation format. It does give credit where credit is due, which is good. However, after the first sentence almost everything else is verbatim, and thus should be presented as a direct quote. Also, this example uses Modern Language Association citation style, not APA (which irritates me). Make sure you follow the style that your instructor wants, not a style you may have previously learned in another class!

What Are the Causes of Plagiarism?

Whether intentional or not, plagiarism happens, and understanding the causes of plagiarism might help you develop strategies to avoid it. Students are motivated to plagiarize for a number of reasons: Some may fear failure or taking risks in writing; others may have inadequate time management skills and think they have no choice but to plagiarize. Other students may believe that the assignment, course, or rules of APA Style and format are unimportant or that the consequences of plagiarism are unimportant or rarely enforced.

To be honest, teachers can be part of the problem as well—some of the causes of plagiarism are linked to the lack of instruction and consistency from faculty members. Instructors need to design writing assignments to minimize the risk or threat of plagiarism (more on this later). Teachers may create assignments that are so generic or like busywork that students feel completing them is a waste of their time, thereby justifying (in students' minds) cheating. Also, teachers and institutions may not consistently report plagiarism when it occurs, penalize it appropriately, or track it over time (Council of Writing Program Administrators, 2003).

How to Avoid Plagiarism

Students and faculty members need to share in the responsibility of taking steps to prevent plagiarism. As a student, you are responsible for your part of this bargain, but know that faculty must also hold up their end of the bargain. Students need to (a) understand that intentional plagiarism harms their character, (b) know that intentional plagiarism cheats themselves, and (c) know that plagiarism is not a practice accepted as a trait of a well-rounded, educated citizen. Faculty members need to demonstrate APA Style and format in the use of internet-based materials, and they need to talk about the underlying implications of plagiarism and what it might mean for a student's future. Faculty members also need to design writing assignments in such a way that the potential for plagiarism is minimized (such as reviewing students' article summaries and rough drafts, examining reference and idea notecards used in writing), and they need to include in their syllabuses the course and university policies on plagiarism (Council of Writing Program Administrators, 2003; Harris, 2005; University of Maryland University College, 2011).

Protecting Yourself From Plagiarism Accusations

There are strategies to help you avoid plagiarism charges. Exhibit 4.4 provides excellent suggestions for protecting yourself from plagiarism.

Unfortunately, if an instructor has been teaching long enough, they have encountered cheating, including plagiarism, in some form or another. The following story demonstrates how important attitude can be and the good that can come from being honest. I once caught two students in an upper division psychology class cheating (it wasn't plagiarism, but copying an assignment). To be honest, intent is sometimes hard to determine even when the instance of cheating is not hard to detect (one student had completed a homework assignment and copied it, and each student put their name on a separate copy). I confronted both students about my discovery. I told them that this was cheating and an act of academic dishonesty and that there would be punishment. One student was extremely remorseful, and after thinking about it, realized what they had done and apologized for it. The other student was offended that they had been called a cheater and expressed no responsibility or remorse for

---

EXHIBIT 4.4. Plagiarism Avoidance: Avoid Being a Victim, Avoid Being Charged With Plagiarism

1. Protect your data and your computer passwords to protect against theft.

2. Do not lend, give, or upload any paper to anyone, even if a student just wants to see what an APA-formatted paper looks like.

3. Report any theft immediately, including to the proper authorities and, in the case of your academic work, your instructors.

4. Save and print all drafts and notes—having your reference, idea notecards, and/or Google Sheets will help support the originality of your written work.

5. Photocopy, print, or save PDFs of all of your sources, and do not cite something that you have not actually read yourself.

6. Be proactive in seeking out the advice of your instructor and teaching assistants. If someone has been reviewing your work all semester, it will be easier for you to make the case that your work is actually your work.

Note. From *Using Sources Effectively: Strengthening Your Writing and Avoiding Plagiarism* (2nd ed.; pp. 24–25), by R. A. Harris, 2005. Copyright 2005 by Pyrczak. Reprinted with permission.

their actions. The former student went on to do great things in our department and was quite successful. The latter student seemed to just fade away. The point of my story is this: How you deal with conditions that tempt you to plagiarize, and your maturity in accepting responsibility for your actions, can make a big difference in how you are perceived by others and the future opportunities you may be afforded. Own your mistakes.

Plagiarism is a form of cheating with serious consequences. I agree with Harris's (2005) statement: "The goal of education is not to get through, but to get better" (p. 15). If you intend to cheat your way through college, why bother? I've been saying to my students for years, would you want to go to the hospital for surgery with a physician who had cheated their way through medical school? Would you want to consult a lawyer who had cheated through law school, or a therapist who had cheated through graduate school? Plagiarism and cheating have the potential to be harmful to others, but most of all they are harmful to you.

QUIZ YOURSELF ON APA STYLE

Because I am not a grammarian, I rely on the advice of others to provide useful tips for avoiding common writing mistakes. There are many good resources available to help you avoid common mistakes (e.g., Bellquist, 1993; Shertzer, 1986). Some are classics, like *The Elements of Style* (Strunk & White, 1979), and there are many updated versions in standalone books, in English books, and on the internet. In Chapters 5 and 6, I present specific instructions and examples of APA Style and format for scientific writing assignments. In this section, I provide numerous helpful resources that you may want to consult when writing and revising your written work. Figure 4.4 contains an example of an exercise I created to help identify APA Style errors. There are many different types of errors. See how many you can find, and then check your work against the errors I found. Figure 4.5 presents my marked-up copy of the exercise. Your instructor may not be as picky as I am, or perhaps they will be pickier. In other words, write for your instructor, because each person has specific likes and dislikes, and as much as we try to objectify the grading of written work, it is very much a subjective process.

Of course, instructors don't always put every comment they want to on student papers because (one hopes) most instructors want to encourage students to work to see improvements in writing and the critical thinking that accompanies it. Table 4.3 includes a list of the 20 most common grammatical errors that occur in student essays (other than misspellings). In this listing based on Connors and Lunsford (1988, as cited in Gottschalk & Hjortshoj, 2004; see also Lunsford, 2005), I provide the error and an example that demonstrates the error. Remember, this is what NOT to do.

As I mentioned earlier, there are many good resources that present detailed information about common mistakes and how to avoid them. Exhibits 4.5 and 4.6 present commonly confused words and commonly misspelled words.

FIGURE 4.4. Sample Paper on Relationship Interactions

Many couples want a successful relationship that is also satisfying. Partners who are satisfied with their interactions tend to be satisfied with other non-romantic relationships (Emmers-Sommer, 514). As a response to ongoing interaction between partners, loving attitudes are formed, things that are shaped by personality type and past and existing relationship interactions (Meeks, Hendrick and Hendrick, '98). That is what my paper is about.

So which aspect of interaction in a relationship is more important; the amount or quality of interaction? Arguments 4 both sides exist.. self-disclosure defined as face—to—face communication of information is often reciprocal, and related to the development of close personal ties (Arliss 1991). Another aspect to examine is if males and females view interaction and relationship quality differently, as suggested by Galliher, Walsh, Rostosky & Kawaguchi (2004): "the domains of couple interaction that predict global relationship quality were different for males and females." (214). Tucker and Anders et al. (1999) report that women have been found to be more satisfied when their partner shows concern with emotional intimacy, but the same has not been found true of men.

A t test was used to examine differences on the agreement scale item "Sharing personal thoughts, feelings, and experiences with my partner improves our relationship," and answers to the yes/no item "Over the duration of my relationship, our physical interaction has increased". A significant relationship exists between "yes" (M-4.43, SD – 0.562) and "no" ($\underline{M}$ = 3.9, $\underline{SD}$ = .65) respondents on self-disclosure scores, $t(4,5) = 2.693$, $p < .05$. There is a statistically significant difference between these groups.

This research done by me stresses the importance of the willingness to self-disclose and encourages positive interaction to achieve relationship satisfaction. LAC issues are proved to be important to consider when pursuing a romantic relationship. Like we talked about in lecture, men and women sometimes want different things out of relationships. Sometimes quality, sometimes quantity. According to John Gottman's website, relationship quality is important.

FIGURE 4.5. Sample Paper on Relationship Interactions, With Instructor Edits

Many couples want a successful relationship that is also satisfying. Partners who are satisfied with their interactions tend to be satisfied with other non-romantic relationships (Emmers-Sommer, ~~514~~2016). As a response to ongoing interaction between partners, loving attitudes are formed, things that are shaped by personality type and past and existing relationship interactions (Meeks~~,~~ ~~et al.~~Hendrick~~, &~~ ~~and~~ Hendrick, ~~'~~1998). ~~That is what my paper is about.~~

Comment: Insert year, not page number

Comment: The word "things" is too vague; try to avoid it when writing scientifically.

Comment: run-on

Comment: Try not to be this informal; your paper is not a conversation between us.

So which aspect of interaction in a relationship is more important~~?~~: the amount or quality of interaction? Arguments ~~for~~4 both sides exist~~.~~ ~~s~~Self-disclosure ~~is~~ defined as face~~—~~-to~~—~~-face communication of information, and it is often reciprocal~~,~~ and related to the development of close personal ties (Arliss, 1991). Another aspect to examine is if males and females view interaction and relationship quality differently, as suggested by Galliher~~, Walsh, Rostosky & Kawaguchi~~ et al. (2004): "~~t~~The domains of couple interaction that predict global relationship quality were different for males and females~~.~~" (p. 214). Tucker ~~and Anders~~et al. (1999) report~~ed~~ that women ~~have been found to be~~are more satisfied when their partner shows concern with emotional intimacy, but the same is not~~has not been found~~ true of men.

A *t* test was used to examine differences on the responses to the agreement scale item "Sharing personal thoughts, feelings, and experiences with my partner improves our relationship," and answers to the yes/no item "Over the duration of my relationship, our physical interaction has increased."~~.~~ A significant ~~relationship~~difference exists between "yes" (M ~~-~~= 4.43, SD ~~-~~= 0.56~~2~~) and "no" (M = 3.9~~4~~, SD = 0.65) participants on self-disclosure scores, $t(4,5)$ = 2.69~~3~~, p ~~<~~= .01~~5~~. There is a statistically significant difference between these groups.

Based on t~~This~~ research, ~~I want to~~ ~~done by me~~ stresses the importance of the willingness to self-disclose and encourages positive interaction to achieve relationship satisfaction. ~~LAC~~ issues ~~are proved~~ to be important to consider when pursuing a romantic relationship. ~~Like we talked about in lecture,~~ men and women sometimes want different ~~things out of~~ outcomes from relationships. ~~Sometimes quality, sometimes quantity.~~ According to ~~John~~ Gottman~~'s website~~ (2018), relationship quality is important.

Comment: Avoid acronyms that make more work for the reader.

Comment: "Prove" is too strong; in science, we don't prove.

Comment: Too informal; and, it appears there is only one author, so there is no "we."

Comment: vague

Comment: This is not a complete sentence, but a sentence fragment.

TABLE 4.3. Grammatical Problems to Avoid

	Twenty most common errors	Example of the error
1.	No comma after an introductory element	Well it wasn't really true.
2.	Vague pronoun reference	John told his father that his car had been stolen.
3.	No comma in compound sentence	I like to eat but I hate to gain weight.
4.	Wrong word	His F in math enhanced his alarm about his D in chemistry.
5.	Missing comma(s) with a nonrestrictive element	The students who had unsuccessfully concealed their participation in the prank were expelled.
6.	Wrong or missing verb ending	I use to go often to town.
7.	Wrong or missing preposition	Cottonwood Grille is located at Boise.
8.	Comma splice	Chloe liked the cat, however, she was allergic to it.
9.	Missing or misplaced possessive apostrophe	Student's backpacks weigh far too much.
10.	Unnecessary shift in tense	I was happily watching TV when suddenly my sister attacks me.
11.	Unnecessary shift in pronoun	When one is tired, you should sleep.
12.	Sentence fragment	He went shopping in the local sports store. An outing he usually enjoyed. [The second part is the fragment.]
13.	Wrong tense or verb form	I would not have said that if I thought it would have shocked her.
14.	Lack of subject–verb agreement	Having many close friends, especially if you've known them for a long time, are a great help in times of trouble.
15.	Missing comma in a series	Students eat, sleep and do homework.
16.	Gender-biased language	When someone plagiarizes from material on a website, he is likely to be caught.
17.	Unnecessary comma(s) with a restrictive element	The novel, that my teacher assigned, was very boring.
18.	Run-on or fused sentence	He loved the seminar he even loved the readings.
19.	Dangling or misplaced modifier	After being put to sleep, a small incision is made below the navel.
20.	*Its–it's* confusion	Its a splendid day for everyone.

Note. Data from Gottschalk and Hjortshoj (2004).

Although there are over 110 different reference formats presented in the *Publication Manual,* the following examples (formatted in APA Style) are from the most common sources that you are likely to cite. Citing electronic documents can be tricky, but the seventh edition of the *Publication Manual* has detailed instructions about how to do this.

EXHIBIT 4.5. Commonly Confused Words

advice/advise	conscience/conscious	hear/here	passed/past
affect/effect	corps/corpse	heard/herd	patience/patients
aisle/isle	council/counsel	hole/whole	peace/piece
allusion/illusion	dairy/diary	human/humane	personal/personnel
an/and	desert/dessert	its/it's	plain/plane
angel/angle	device/devise	know/no	precede/proceed
ascent/assent	die/dye	later/latter	presence/presents
bare/bear	dominant/dominate	lay/lie	principal/principle
brake/break	elicit/illicit	lead/led	quiet/quite
breath/breathe	eminent/immanent/ imminent	lessen/lesson	rain/reign/rein
buy/by		loose/lose	raise/raze
capital/capitol	envelop/envelope	may be/maybe	reality/realty
choose/chose	every day/everyday	miner/minor	respectfully/ respectively
cite/sight/site	fair/fare	moral/morale	
complement/ compliment	formally/formerly	of/off	reverend/reverent
	forth/fourth		

Note. From *The Psychology Student Writer's Manual* (2nd ed., pp. 52–54), by J. M. Scott, R. Koch, G. M. Scott, and S. M. Garrison, 2002, Pearson Education. Copyright 2002 by Pearson Education. Reprinted with permission.

Journal Article

Fouad, N. A., Grus, C. L., Hatcher, R. L., Kaslow, N. J., Hutchings, P. S., Madson, M. B., Collins, F. L., & Crossman, R. E. (2009). Competency benchmarks: A model for understanding and measuring competence in professional psychology across training levels. *Training and Education in Professional Psychology, 3*(Suppl.), S5–S26. https://doi.org/10.1037/a0015832

Freeman, S., Eddy, S. L., McDonough, M., Smith, M. K., Okoroafor, N., Jordt, H., & Wenderoth, M. P. (2014). Active learning increases student performance in science, engineering, and mathematics. *PNAS, 111*(23), 8410–8415.

Gurung, R. A. R., Hackathorn, J., Enns, C., Frantz, S., Cacioppo, J. T., Loop, T., & Freeman, J. E. (2016). Strengthening introductory psychology: A new model for teaching the introductory course. *American Psychologist, 71*(2), 112–124. https://doi.org/10.1037/a0040012

Holdhus, K., Hoisaeter, S., Maeland, K., Vangsnes, V., Engelsen, K. S., Espenland, M., & Espeland, A. (2016). Improvisation in teaching and education—Roots and applications. *Teacher Education & Development, 3*(1204142). https://doi.org/10.1080/2331186x.2016.1204142

Book

Gabriel, K. F. (2008). *Teaching unprepared students: Strategies for promoting success and retention in higher education.* Stylus Publishing.

Hettich, P. I., & Landrum, R. E. (2014). *Your undergraduate degree in psychology: From college to career.* Sage.

EXHIBIT 4.6. Commonly Misspelled Words

a lot	fascinate	occasionally	scenery
acceptable	finally	occurred	science
accessible	foresee	occurrences	secede
accommodate	forty	omission	secession
accompany	fulfill	omit	secretary
accustomed	gauge	opinion	senseless
acquire	guaranteed	opponent	separate
against	guard	parallel	sergeant
annihilate	harass	parole	shining
apparent	hero	peaceable	significant
arguing	heroes	performance	sincerely
argument	humorous	pertain	skiing
authentic	hurried	practical	stubbornness
before	hurriedly	preparation	studying
begin	hypocrite	probably	succeed
beginning	ideally	process	success
believe	immediately	professor	successfully
benefited	immense	prominent	susceptible
bulletin	incredible	pronunciation	suspicious
business	innocuous	psychology	technical
cannot	intercede	publicly	temporary
category	interrupt	pursue	tendency
committee	irrelevant	pursuing	therefore
condemn	irresistible	questionnaire	tragedy
courteous	irritate	realize	truly
definitely	knowledge	receipt	tyranny
dependent	license	received	unanimous
desperate	likelihood	recession	unconscious
develop	maintenance	recommend	undoubtedly
different	manageable	referring	until
disappear	meanness	religious	vacuum
disappoint	mischievous	remembrance	valuable
easily	missile	reminisce	various
efficient	necessary	repetition	vegetable
environment	nevertheless	representative	visible
equipped	no one	rhythm	without
exceed	noticeable	ridiculous	women
exercise	noticing	roommate	writing
existence	nuisance	satellite	
experience	occasion	scarcity	

Note. From *The Psychology Student Writer's Manual* (2nd ed., pp. 52–54), by J. M. Scott, R. Koch, G. M. Scott, and S. M. Garrison, 2002, Pearson Education. Copyright 2002 by Pearson Education. Reprinted with permission.

Edited Book

Brakke, K., & Houska, J. A. (Eds.). (2015). *Telling stories: The art and science of storytelling as an instructional strategy*. Society for the Teaching of Psychology. http://teachpsych.org/ebooks/tellingstories.html

Chastain, G., & Landrum, R. E. (Eds.). (1999). *Protecting human subjects: Departmental subject pools and institutional review boards*. American Psychological Association.

Halpern, D. F. (Ed.). (2010). *Undergraduate education in psychology: A blueprint for the future of the discipline*. American Psychological Association.

Chapter in Edited Book

Kezar, A., & Holcombe, E. (2016). Institutional transformation in STEM: Insights from change research and the Keck-PKAL project. In G. C. Weaver, W. D. Burgess, A. L. Childress, & L. Slakey (Eds.), *Transforming institutions: Undergraduate STEM education for the 21ˢᵗ century* (pp. 35–47). Purdue University Press.

Landrum, R. E., Beins, B. C., Bhalla, M., Brakke, K., Briihl, D. S., Curl-Langager, R. M., Pusateri, T. P., & Van Kirk, J. J. (2010). Desired outcomes of an undergraduate education in psychology from departmental, student, and societal perspectives. In D. F. Halpern (Ed.), *Undergraduate education in psychology: A blueprint for the future of the discipline* (pp. 145–160). American Psychological Association.

Conference Presentation

Brakke, K., & Landrum, R. E. (2019, October 8–10). *Storytelling startup: How to incorporate story in the psychology classroom* [Workshop]. STP Annual Conference on Teaching, Denver, CO, United States. https://teachpsych.org/Conference-Schedule

Landrum, R. E. (2019, August 8-11). *Thirty years teaching psychology: Lessons learnt (…and those not so much…)* [American Psychological Foundation Charles L. Brewer Distinguished Teaching of Psychology Award Invited Address]. American Psychological Association, Chicago, IL, United States. http://app.core-apps.com/apa2019/event/4d029ea838ad25ed69714ffcfb5d16a3

Magazine or Newspaper Article

Lin, L., Christidis, P., & Stamm, K. (2017, October 8). The path to becoming a psychologist. *Monitor on Psychology, 48*(9), 17.

Selingo, J. J. (2013, April 29). Does the college major matter? Not really. *The New York Times*. https://thechoice.blogs.nytimes.com/2013/04/29/does-the-college-major-matter-not-really/?mcubz=3

Sevener, J. (2014, February 7). 10 reasons for teachers to use improv in the classroom. *The Second City*. https://www.secondcity.com/network/network10-reasons-teachers-use-improv-classroom/

Internet Material

American Psychological Association. (2013). *APA guidelines for the undergraduate psychology major: Version 2.0*. https://www.apa.org/ed/precollege/about/undergraduate-major

National Center for Education Statistics. (2017). *Degrees in psychology conferred by postsecondary institutions, by level of degree and sex of student: Selected years, 1945-50 through 2014-15* [Table 325.80]. https://nces.ed.gov/programs/digest/d16/tables/dt16_325.80.asp?current=yes

U.S. Department of Labor. (2017). *O*NET Online*. https://www.onetonline.org/

Vita, M. (n.d.). *Distinguishing correlational vs. experimental research*. American Psychological Association, Project Assessment. http://pass.apa.org/docs/distinguishing-correlational-vs-experimental-research/

5

Bringing the Audience Up to Speed With Literature Reviews

Writing is hard work. A clear sentence is no accident. Very few sentences come out right the first time, or even the third time. Remember this in moments of despair. If you find that writing is hard, it's because it is hard.

—WILLIAM ZINSSER, *ON WRITING WELL: THE CLASSIC GUIDE TO WRITING NONFICTION*

The last chapter ended with information about plagiarism and how to avoid it. Focusing now on the positive, you need the skills and abilities to be able to research a paper, extract key notes, draw conclusions, analyze and synthesize, and so forth. Collegiate writing assignments are precisely designed to aid in the development of all those skills, not merely to create a "paper." In this chapter, I discuss literature reviews and term papers.

LITERATURE REVIEWS PROVIDE STORY CONTEXT

Literature is a fairly generic term that can be used in a number of contexts. First, a student could write a literature review (or lit review, or review of the literature). This entails an integrated synopsis or summary of some aspect of the psychological literature related to a variable or behavior of interest. In addition, the literature review is often a key component of the Introduction section of a research paper or a lab report. Furthermore, depending on how your instructor defines it, a review of the literature could be a key component of a term paper. Given the importance of reviewing the literature and the many variations of it that appear in scientific writing, it is worthwhile to spend some time discussing how to write a literature review.

A literature review is meant to do just that—review the existing literature relevant to the topic you are studying. A review article is intended to be broad—that is, a comprehensive review of the published literature in a particular area, providing the reader a chance to describe what is known and to determine what is next.

Eisenberg (2000) described four common types of review articles—those that (a) generate new knowledge, (b) test a theory, (c) integrate theories, and (d) develop and evaluate a new theory.

However, a more common type of literature review is one that is embedded in a larger paper, such as a research paper. A literature review accomplishes much more than just summarizing the literature (University of Melbourne, n.d.); for instance, a literature review provides a historical overview of the topic, presents earlier theories, and also provides background on the purpose of the review (i.e., point of view). A well-written literature review helps the reader understand disagreements and debates about the topic in context and also identifies gaps, omissions, and unanswered questions in previous work. Finally, a literature review highlights exemplary or seminal studies in a research area, identifies patterns or trends in the literature, and—very important for students—demonstrates your knowledge and skill. This chapter describes the process of reviewing the literature, which requires the writer to integrate all the scientific writing concepts and skills mentioned so far.

GUIDING PRINCIPLES FOR WRITING LITERATURE REVIEWS

Galvan (2006) offered a comprehensive set of writing instructions for literature reviews. You begin by identifying the broad problem area (e.g., landfills are filling at an exponential rate) but avoid global statements (e.g., recycling is important). Early in the review, indicate why the topic being reviewed is important—if you don't convince the reader that the topic is important, then why should they bother reading the review? Distinguish between research findings (such as journal articles) and other sources of information (such as the opinions of politicians or popular media reports), and be sure to identify a classic or landmark study as such. Sometimes you'll hear these types of studies referred to as *seminal studies,* and the ability to point this out makes you a savvy researcher. You also provide a great service to your reader when you can identify why a particular study is important.

If you are commenting on the timeliness of a topic, you will want to be specific in describing the time frame; this gives the reader some context and explains why it is an important detail. If there are other literature reviews relevant to your topic, be sure to mention them, even if you are not discussing those other reviews in detail. Be careful about making statements such as "No studies have ever been conducted on this topic." You cannot be certain of that statement—many studies have been conducted by researchers and never been published, and a major reason for nonpublication is that no significant results were found. Or maybe there are studies about that topic available, but they are not published in the English language, or not indexed in the databases that you searched. What would be better to say is this: "To my knowledge, there are no published studies available on this topic."

Avoid long lists of nonspecific references. Sometimes students (and experienced researchers) want to either (a) show off their scholarly work by citing every study they reviewed, whether it is relevant or not, or (b) conserve space by citing multiple studies at the end of a sentence or paragraph. There is no exact number of studies that should be cited in a literature review—the goal is to provide a thorough overview of the topic being studied, and that could require any number of studies, depending on the context, the instructor, the type of assignment, and so on. If the results of previous studies are inconsistent or vary widely, cite them separately. This actually helps lay the foundation for the later parts of your Introduction section, in which you describe a conflict or gap in the literature, that is, an unresolved question to be answered. Identifying inconsistencies in the literature helps emphasize the need for your work.

REASSEMBLING PIECES OF THE STORY: SYNTHESIS

The analysis, synthesis, and evaluation components of the literature review are all key. Using the notecard method, you will have already analyzed each of the articles you think should be included in your review. That analysis is important, but not enough. You must then synthesize the main ideas presented in the literature with a critical, evaluative viewpoint. This is a skill that everyone has to work at to acquire, and just like any skill, it takes time and practice.

Based on an idea from Reaves (2004), I created the materials in Figures 5.1 and 5.2 to demonstrate the importance of synthesis. In Figure 5.1, analysis and extraction have been completed, and a summary of each study outcome has been generated, but the product looks more like book report summaries than an integrated review of the literature. It looks as if the author picked up a stack of idea notecards from each source and wrote an individual paragraph about each. Although analysis is present, there is no synthesis. Synthesis means seeking out underlying themes to see connections across studies, not just analyzing differences between them. Figure 5.2 demonstrates a smoother, synthesized review of the literature that was adapted from Landrum, Gurung, and Amsel (2019). Notice that the text is much shorter, and also notice how references about a particular theme have been grouped together. The intellectual benefit of a well-written literature review is that the author has completed this complex task of analysis–synthesis–evaluation for you and thus provided a rich context for understanding the complexity of a particular psychological idea.

FIGURE 5.1. Sample Literature Review on Introductory Psychology Courses, Without Synthesis (continues)

The introductory psychology course is an important course to teach, and a great deal of research has been conducted about this course over time. In thinking about what chapters should be taught in the course, Weiten and Wight (1992) did extensive work to help understand the typical teaching model used by examining the evolution of introductory psychology textbooks.

A different approach was taken by other researchers to examine what is taught in introductory psychology at a more granular level. Quereshi and Sackett (1977) conducted a survey in introductory psychology instructors and asked them about the desirable features of an introductory psychology textbook in hopes of developing an aid or rubric in helping instructors select textbooks.

When Quereshi (1993) examined the contents of 60 introductory psychology textbooks in a 7-year span compared to 52 textbooks published in the following 10-year span, the more recent introductory psychology textbooks were longer, more comprehensive, and judged to be more readable.

In an attempt to identify, understand, and update those core concepts in introductory psychology, Zechmeister and Zechmeister (2000) examined the glossaries of 10 introductory psychology textbooks and identified 2,505 different concepts and terms across all books. However, only 64 items appeared in all 10 glossaries, and half of all the items (2,505 items) appeared in only one glossary/textbook.

How the course is organized is only one method of examining the introductory psychology course in American psychology. Batsell et al. (2016) studied the efficacy of the testing effect in an introductory psychology classroom and found that quiz performance was enhanced compared to a control group.

Another interesting study was performed by Cathey, Visio, Whisenhunt, Hudson and Shoptaugh (2016) when they offered study skills training sessions at the midterm examination point in their large enrollment introductory psychology course. Students who self-selected into the training sessions had lower pre-session exam scores, and by the end of the semester these pre-existing differences were eliminated compared to a control group.

FIGURE 5.1. Sample Literature Review on Introductory Psychology Courses, Without Synthesis (continued)

What is the effect of implementing team-based learning across multiple sections using multiple instructors? When Travis, Hudson, Hendricks-Lepp, Street, and Weidenbenner (2016) did this in introductory psychology courses using common midterm and final exams and common mid-semester and end-of-semester student satisfaction surveys, they report that team-based learning is more effective than lecture when contributing to learning with no decrement in student satisfaction scores.

FIGURE 5.2. Sample Literature Review on Introductory Psychology Courses, With Synthesis

For many educators, the ultimate utility of the accumulation of evidence derived from research about the introductory psychology course revolves around teaching and learning; this is plain but not so simple. Discussions about and research concerning the content of what should be covered in the introductory psychology course have been ongoing for some time (Weiten & Wight, 1992), and have led to the recent emergence of the common core model for the course. For instance, there have been numerous efforts to identify core concepts in the introductory psychology course (Quereshi, 1993; Quereshi & Sackett, 1977; Zechmeister & Zechmeister, 2000). A host of other approaches, however, reinforce the importance and prevalence in the practical teaching and learning aspects of introductory psychology. For example, researchers have examined the role of quizzing in introductory psychology (Batsell et al., 2016), studied helping students improve study skills for a midterm exam (Cathey et al., 2016), and examined how to teach the introductory course using team-based learning (Travis et al., 2016).

Note. From "The Importance of Taking Psychology: A Comparison of Three Levels of Exposure," by R. E. Landrum, R. A. R. Gurung, and E. Amsel, 2019, *Teaching of Psychology, 46*(4), p. 291 (https://doi.org/10.1177/0098628319872574). Copyright 2019 by Sage. Adapted with permission.

ORGANIZING A LITERATURE REVIEW

Depending on the course, instructor, and assignment, you may be asked to write a stand-alone literature review paper, as described previously. However, a more common type of literature review may be embedded in a larger paper, such as a research paper. This type of literature review might be for a research methods or experimental design class. In this case, the literature review is actually part of the Introduction section, which is part of a larger manuscript.

In the following paragraphs, I present the instructions that I give to students when I assign a literature review as part of the Introduction section of a research paper. Depending on the assignment, you may be asked to follow a similar set of instructions. Generally, your literature review will be organized like this: (a) introduce the topic and the research question, stating why both are important; (b) narrow the research question or studies to be discussed; (c) provide a brief outline or synopsis of the paper; (d) describe the studies in some detail; (e) compare and evaluate studies; and (f) discuss the implications of the studies (University of Washington, 2017). Although I have customized my instructions over the years, they originally came from an earlier edition of Bordens and Abbott (2004).

Introduce the Topic

Introduce the reader to the issue in the first paragraph by defining or identifying the general topic. Convince the reader that this is an important issue. Perhaps it affects a large number of people or is an essential component of daily life. Try to impress upon the reader why this topic is so important that it warrants the effort and resources necessary to conduct research. Kendall et al. (2000) offered specific ideas for the opening paragraph, such as

- asking a rhetorical question that helps readers think about how they feel about an issue

- sharing an everyday experience that is common to many individuals

- using an analogy that grabs the reader's attention in an interesting fashion

- providing a striking statistical fact that surprises the reader and makes them intrigued to learn more

- alluding to a historical event that still has relevance in the present day and is worthy of continued study

- alerting the reader to an under-studied area or newly emerging area in psychology where new research efforts are warranted.

Review the Literature

Review the available literature on the topic. If there are studies related specifically to your topic, present them here. If there are no specific studies, broaden your review of the literature to include related areas. Show that you have done your scholarly homework, and provide a context for your study. Point out overall trends in the published literature about this topic, using analysis, synthesis, and your idea notecards or Google Sheets. Group the research studies and other types of literature according to common threads such as qualitative versus quantitative, objectives, methodology, and so forth. Discuss the general outcomes of each study and not the methodological details, unless those details are vital to your study.

Identify the Problem or Gap in Knowledge

Within this context, identify a problem or area in which the knowledge is incomplete. This becomes your statement of the problem to be addressed by your research. You have reviewed the literature and discovered a gap—an unresolved problem or issue. (If this were a TV or movie script, it would be setting up the conflict between the main characters.) The goal of your study is to fill that gap (resolve the conflict). Explain why your study is important within the context of previous studies and the unanswered question.

State Your Purpose

Provide a clear statement of purpose for the current study. Be specific about the problem you are going to solve. Tell why this study is necessary to fill this gap in the research. In fact, it is often a good idea to signal this by including a sentence that begins "The purpose of my study is to. . . ."

Preview the Study ("Coming Attractions")

Next, give a brief overview of the methodology that will be used to address the knowledge gap. This should be just a snapshot of the participants, materials, and basic procedure used in the study.

Narrow Your Focus

What do you expect to happen? If you are writing a broad literature review, your paper will likely end with conclusions and recommendations for future researchers. However, if you are conducting a research project, you can conclude your Introduction section with the expected outcomes of the specific hypotheses to be tested. Develop your working hypotheses on the basis of your expectations and your review of the literature. Be as specific as possible. Well-written hypotheses actually provide guidance later as you determine the statistical approach you will take in analyzing your results. Good science requires that hypotheses be testable—your wording is essential here. A good hypothesis is also clearly related to the statement of purpose (described previously) and helps the researcher design an interesting study, regardless of whether the hypothesis is rejected or fails to be rejected.

The Introduction is just the first part of a research paper (I address all the major parts of the research paper in Chapter 6). A common analogy for a research paper is an hourglass, in which the Introduction makes up most of the top half (see Figure 5.3). As you can see, both the hourglass and the Introduction section start very broad and then become more narrow and focused. After narrowing, there will again be a broadening of approach in the Discussion section.

FIGURE 5.3. Hourglass Model

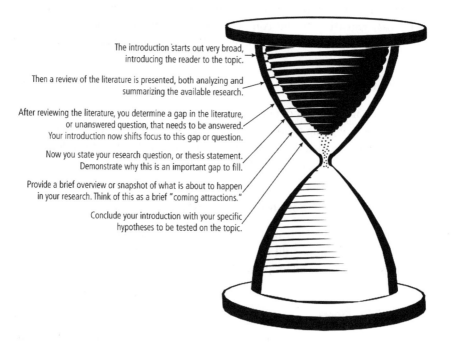

The introduction starts out very broad, introducing the reader to the topic.

Then a review of the literature is presented, both analyzing and summarizing the available research.

After reviewing the literature, you determine a gap in the literature, or unanswered question, that needs to be answered. Your introduction now shifts focus to this gap or question.

Now you state your research question, or thesis statement. Demonstrate why this is an important gap to fill.

Provide a brief overview or snapshot of what is about to happen in your research. Think of this as a brief "coming attractions."

Conclude your introduction with your specific hypotheses to be tested on the topic.

SAMPLE LITERATURE REVIEW

In this section, I present an actual first draft of a literature review written by one of my students, Izzy (I have used this work, and her name, with Izzy's permission). When I say actual first draft, I should qualify that. Izzy is a very good student and a very good writer, and she agreed to share this work with me for this book. However, there are not that many errors in her first rough draft, which is, of course, a tribute to her work. Thus, you will see three variations presented: an original rough draft (Figure 5.4); this rough draft marked the way I would have marked it (Figure 5.5); and the final draft (Figure 5.6).

First look at Figure 5.4, then look at Figure 5.5 with my editing marks. This is an interesting exercise in a number of ways. First, editing is often subjective; I made suggestions to Izzy's paper that I thought would improve it. These weren't errors, per se, but stylistic suggestions. Second, another faculty member (or you, for that matter) might mark this paper quite differently than I did. I probably let some things go that others would not. For instance, the last part of the Introduction uses the future tense. This was okay with me because during the class, students wrote their Introduction sections before they had conducted their study. Now look at the finished product in Figure 5.6.

If you closely compare the edited draft with the final draft, you will note that Izzy did not make all the corrections I suggested, which is fine. She also corrected some items I did not point out. This constant revising and editing is all part of the process of scientific writing in psychology.

How did Izzy do with respect to the criteria from Galvan (2006) I presented earlier? In looking at the first draft of Izzy's Introduction, it's well organized. Izzy did plenty of background research on the topic, and when she was enrolled in the course in fall 2018, most of her reference citations were current and up-to-date. She made the effort to thoroughly explain her ideas and back up those ideas with citations from previous work, which is why her efforts earned distinguished marks. But please note that it is not included here as an example of a perfect paper. The three manuscripts presented here are intended to demonstrate the value of writing and receiving comments on a first draft, as well as the improvements that can be made in one's writing (in a relatively short amount of time) for the final draft. In the next chapter, the story we started with the literature review will be continued in the context of a complete research paper.

FIGURE 5.4. Sample Literature Review on Social Media Effects, Rough Draft (continues)

The Effects of Social Media Use on Depression

A compelling statistic that is not overly surprising is that more than 70 percent of youth and young adults who use the Internet use social media sites (Davila, et al., 2012). Social media sites and social networking sites, or SNS, range from colloquial use to professional use, as well as contemporary designs to platforms meant for professional networking. Common platforms used for studies include Instagram, Twitter, Facebook, and LinkedIn. LinkedIn is the most commonly used professional social networking cite (Jones, Colditz, Sidani, Lin, Terry, & Primack, 2016). Similarly, about 90 percent of 13-29 year olds (of Internet users in the U.S.) have at least one social networking site (Cavazos-Rehg, Krauss, Sowles, Connolly, Rosas, Bharadwaj, Grocza, & Bierut., 2017). With the rise of social media and SNS, many researchers show interest in possible psychological problems that may also arise with the decrease of face-to-face communication, particularly in the pervasiveness of depression.

A review of literature demonstrates the prevalence of depression, as well as the possible relationships between depression and the use of social media. According to one study, participants who used LinkedIn at a minimum of once per week had significantly greater chances of increased depression in comparison to the participants who did not use LinkedIn (Jones, et al., 2016). Depressive symptoms appear in non-professional platforms as well. For instance, another group of researchers discussed the most popular observed theme from a sample of 2,739 depression-related posts on Tumblr, and these themes found were: self-loathing, loneliness/feeling unloved, and self-harm and/or scars from self-harm (Cavazos-Rehg, et al., 2017). Similarly, Twitter users expressing dissatisfaction more commonly use swear words to convey negative emotion, anger, sadness, and sexuality than other users. (Yang & Srinivasan, 2016). On another note, if you search for the terms "depressed," "suicide," "self-mutilation," or "cutting," Tumblr will first send you to a screen with suggestions for seeking help (Cavazos-Rehg, et al., 2017). Researchers from each

FIGURE 5.4. Sample Literature Review on Social Media Effects, Rough Draft (continued)

of these studies emphasize the significance of depression existing across social

media platforms, both professional and entertainment-based. The real question

behind the compilation of all this research asks to what extent depression exists

and if there is an actual relationship between usage of social media and

increased depressive symptoms.

Many researchers believe in the existence of a connection between

depression and the use of social media or SNS; however, uncertainty still

remains due to the varying topics of research in this field, which tend to lead to

inconsistent or incomparable results. Researchers in this field, for example,

analyze the number of virtual friends an individual has, as well as the types of

posts that are most common within platforms, in an attempt to reduce the

number of variables that might contribute to a possible relationship. Another

group of researchers took a more specific approach to interactions online, and

examined more than merely the association between time spent on social

media and depression, but also took into consideration the quality of

interactions the participants engaged in. The authors of this study found that

corumination, or the act of talking about problems with friends in a negative

and repetitive way, can actually predict increases in depressive symptoms

(Davila, et al., 2012). Finding connections between quality of interactions and

frequency of depressive symptoms expands the dimensions in which social

media possibly affects individuals, and leads to development of more theories.

Other psychologists consider the number of followers (i.e., friends on

Facebook, followers on Instagram) an individual has on social media sites.

Researchers found that "...the average time spent on Instagram correlated

positively with depressive symptoms, trait anxiety, social comparison

orientation, physical appearance anxiety, and body image disturbance"

(Sherlock & Wagstaff, 2018, p. 6). The idea that social media, in this case

Instagram, affects more than just depressive symptoms, but also affects an

individual's self-image and body image leads to more questions about exactly

FIGURE 5.4. Sample Literature Review on Social Media Effects, Rough Draft (continued)

how much of our lives can be affected by social media. Similarly, researchers from a separate study who also analyzed number of followers found that number of followers correlated positively with depression and trait anxiety. These researchers found a negative correlation between number of followers and self-esteem (Sherlock & Wagstaff, 2018). The results are inconsistent, as the higher the number of followers actually correlates with a lower level of self-esteem. Number of followers is one way to analyze the effect of social media on its users; even so, research on the content of posts suggests another outlet for depressive symptoms.

More experts in social media insist that content of posts, or status updates, should be a priority in identifying important components of social media or the individual that add to the intensity of depressive symptoms. One researcher analyzed the specific types of status updates on Facebook. According to this research, there are three note-worthy forms of "status updates" on Facebook: updates that reveal low negative self-esteem, self-promoting updates, and self-important/narrow-minded posts (Blease, 2015). Analyzing depression from this angle becomes possible after establishing criteria behind each type of status update. Another important variable needing to be defined is the scientific term for happiness, referred to as Subjective well-being, or SWB. The presence of positive emotions, the absence of negative emotions, and life satisfaction of the individual determine SWB (Yang & Srinivasan, 2016). By measuring SWB, researchers effectively evaluate the overall mood or possible prevalence of depressive symptoms. Equally as important, self-esteem can be described as "the evaluative component of the self—the degree to which one prizes, values, approves or likes oneself" (Pantic, 2014, p. 653). Types of posts, SWB, and self-esteem are all components that define how an individual sees himself or herself, and ultimately predict levels of depressive moods within social media sites.

FIGURE 5.4. Sample Literature Review on Social Media Effects, Rough Draft (continued)

Many researchers interested in the relationship between social media use and depression, as well as other psychological disorders, have performed studies in an effort to find a correlation; however, results vary drastically. Some researchers found that the presence of increased communication or increased number "friends," positively affect mood. These such studies posit that the absence of face-to-face interactions may make it easier to interact with other people, particularly for shy individuals or persons who often feel lonely (Brailovskaia & Margraf, 2016), which explains, to an extent, the conflicting results across studies. Conversely, other researchers find the opposite: that increased use of social networking negatively affects young adults' abilities to interact face to face and demonstrate more depressive symptoms. On a similar note, research analyzing body image and gender in comparison to social media use also demonstrates high levels of depressive symptoms. Strubel, Petrie, and Pookulnagara in their 2018 study defined social media as having become a form of sociocultural channel that transits body-centric information more than previous media outlets. Prior to social media and SNS, there were limited ways for individuals' body-image and self-esteem to be influenced. Social media and SNS are a newly developed, *highly effective* form of reinforcing hegemonic norms, particularly those that reiterate the ideal body image for both men and women. The authors of this study focused on the body dissatisfaction women have when they compare themselves to the ideal bodies represented consistently across social media platforms. The authors explain that the internalization of such ideals may lead to negative emotions, such as shame, guilt, anger, and sadness among these women.

However varying or contradicting prior results may be, a consistent thread weaves across all studies: social media use and SNS use significantly impact individual mood. In order to fill the knowledge gap, I examine the relationship between possible existing depression and the use of social media, without emphasis on specific depressive symptoms or direct analysis of number

FIGURE 5.4. Sample Literature Review on Social Media Effects, Rough Draft (continued)

of followers. The purpose of my study is to determine if there is a relationship between depression and the use of social media.

To research the possible relationship between depression and social media use, a sample of undergraduate students participated in a survey. The sample was taken from Introduction to Psychology students at Boise State University, and participants responded to compilation of several research surveys. To measure possible correlations, evaluative questions concerning the presence of depressive symptoms, as well as questions measuring the amount of media use, were presented in survey form.

Upon review of previous literature and research performed regarding social media, SNS, and various levels or types of depressive symptoms on individuals, I expect that this study will reproduce the most typical results found so far. The more an individual uses social media, regardless of the platform, the more that individual will experience increased levels of depression. I hypothesize, first, that there will be a positive correlation between depression and the use of social media. Second, I hypothesize that the platform through which an individual accesses social media or SNS will not matter; the quantifiable amount of use will be the predictor of depressive symptoms and level of depression.

Note. From course literature review by Izzy Riley, 2018. Copyright 2018 by Izzy Riley. Printed with permission.

FIGURE 5.5. Sample Literature Review on Social Media Effects, With Instructor Edits (continues)

The Effects of Social Media Use on Depression

~~A compelling statistic that is not overly surprising is that m~~More than 70 percent of youth and young adults who use the Internet use social media sites (Davila~~,~~ et al., 2012). Social media sites and social networking sites ~~(, or~~ SNS)~~,~~ range from colloquial use to professional use, as well as contemporary designs to platforms meant for professional networking. Common platforms used for studies include Instagram, Twitter, Facebook, and LinkedIn. LinkedIn is the most commonly used professional social networking cite (Jones et al., ~~Colditz, Sidani,~~ ~~Lin, Terry, & Primack,~~ 2016). Similarly, about 90-~~%~~percent of 13- to 29--year- olds (of ~~I~~internet users in the U.S.) have at least one social networking site (Cavazos-Rehg~~, Krauss, Sowles, Connolly, Rosas, Bharadwaj, Grocza, & Bierut,~~ et al., 2017). With the rise of social media and SNS, many researchers show interest in possible psychological problems that may also arise with the decrease of face-to-face communication, particularly in the pervasiveness of depression.

> **Comment:** Page number is missing from inside top margin (should be flush right).
>
> **Formatted:** Font: (Default) +Body (Calibri), 11 pt, Bold
>
> **Formatted:** Font: 11 pt, Bold
>
> **Formatted:** Font: (Default) +Body (Calibri), 11 pt, Bold

A review of literature demonstrates the prevalence of depression, as well as the possible relationships between depression and the use of social media. According to one ~~study~~researcher, participants who used LinkedIn at a minimum of once per week had significantly greater chances of increased depression in comparison to the participants who did not use LinkedIn (Jones, et al., 2016). Depressive symptoms appear in non-professional online platforms as well. For instance, another group of researchers discussed the most popular observed theme from a sample of 2,739 depression-related posts on Tumblr, and these themes found were: self-loathing, loneliness/feeling unloved, and self-harm and/or scars from self-harm (Cavazos-Rehg, et al., 2017). Similarly, Twitter users expressing dissatisfaction more commonly use swear words to convey negative emotion, anger, sadness, and sexuality than other users~~;~~ (Yang & Srinivasan, 2016). On another note, if you search for the terms "depressed," "suicide," "self-mutilation," or "cutting," Tumblr will first send you to a screen with suggestions for seeking help (Cavazos-Rehg~~,~~ et al., 2017). Researchers from each of these studies emphasize the significance of depression existing across social media platforms, both professional and entertainment-based. The real question behind the compilation of all this research asks to what extent depression exists and if there is an actual relationship between usage of social media and increased depressive symptoms.

> **Comment:** But what is the urgent problem? Yes, many people use the Internet. But this first paragraph does not signal to me the key issue that is about to be addressed in this research. By the end of the paragraph, I should have a good sense of what's coming.
>
> **Comment:** This is the pathetic fallacy error--literature cannot demonstrate.
>
> **Comment:** Awkward phrasing; did you mean to write "and these themes were found"?
>
> **Comment:** This is a nice summary, except for the pathetic fallacy error -- the question cannot ask.

FIGURE 5.5. Sample Literature Review on Social Media Effects, With Instructor Edits (continued)

Many researchers believe in the existence of a connection between depression and the use of social media or SNS; however, uncertainty still remains due to the varying topics of research in this field, which tend to lead to inconsistent or incomparable results. Researchers in this field, for example, analyze the number of virtual friends an individual has, as well as the types of posts that are most common within platforms, in an attempt to reduce the number of variables that might contribute to a possible relationship. Another group of researchers took a more specific approach to interactions online, and examined more than merely the association between time spent on social media and depression, but also took into consideration the quality of interactions the participants engaged in. The authors of this study found that corumination, or the act of talking about problems with friends in a negative and repetitive way, can actually predict increases in depressive symptoms (Davila, et al., 2012). Finding connections between quality of interactions and frequency of depressive symptoms expands the dimensions in which social media possibly affects individuals, and leads to development of more theories.

Other psychologists consider the number of followers (i.e., friends on Facebook, followers on Instagram) an individual has on social media sites. Researchers found that "…the average time spent on Instagram correlated positively with depressive symptoms, trait anxiety, social comparison orientation, physical appearance anxiety, and body image disturbance" (Sherlock & Wagstaff, 2018, p. 6). The idea that social media, in this case Instagram, affects more than just depressive symptoms, but also affects an individual's self-image and body image, leads to more questions about exactly how much of our lives can be affected by social media. Similarly, researchers from a separate study who also analyzed number of followers found that number of followers correlated positively with depression and trait anxiety. These researchers found a negative correlation between number of followers and self-esteem (Sherlock & Wagstaff, 2018). The results are inconsistent, as the higher the number of followers actually correlates with a lower level of self-esteem. Number of followers is one way to analyze the effect of social media on its users; even so, research on the content of posts suggests another outlet for depressive symptoms.

More experts in social media insist that content of posts, or status updates, should be a priority in identifying important components of social

Comment: Either use the entire phrase or the acronym, but do not use both.

Comment: Nice; you are setting up the gap, the conflict.

Comment: It looks like this word is spelled with a hyphen, such as co-rumination.

Comment: This section mentioned one group of researchers, then another group of researchers, but there is only one citation, so there seems to be a citation missing.

Comment: You have fallen into the habit of always citing your authors at the end of the sentence. You can also open the sentence with the researcher's names; this will provide some variety to your sentence structures.

Comment: Pathetic fallacy error; research does not suggest.

FIGURE 5.5. Sample Literature Review on Social Media Effects, With Instructor Edits (continued)

---

media or the individual that add to the intensity of depressive symptoms. Blease (2015) ~~One researcher~~ analyzed the specific types of status updates on Facebook. According to this research, there are three note-worthy forms of "status updates" on Facebook: updates that reveal low negative self-esteem, self-promoting updates, and self-important/narrow-minded posts ~~(Blease, 2015)~~. Analyzing depression from this angle becomes possible after establishing criteria behind each type of status update. Another important variable needing to be defined is the scientific term for happiness, referred to as ~~Subjective~~ subjective well-being, or SWB. The presence of positive emotions, the absence of negative emotions, and life satisfaction of the individual determine SWB (Yang & Srinivasan, 2016). By measuring SWB, researchers effectively evaluate the overall mood or possible prevalence of depressive symptoms. Equally as important, self-esteem can be described as "the evaluative component of the self—the degree to which one prizes, values, approves or likes oneself" (Pantic, 2014, p. 653). Types of posts, SWB, and self-esteem are all components that define how an individual sees himself or herself, and ultimately predict levels of depressive moods within social media sites.

> Comment: Just as an example...

Many researchers are interested in the relationship between social media use and depression, as well as other psychological disorders, and they have performed studies in an effort to find a correlation; however, results vary drastically. Some researchers found that the presence of increased communication or increased number "friends," positively affect mood. These such studies posit that the absence of face-to-face interactions may make it easier to interact with other people, particularly for shy individuals or persons who often feel lonely (Brailovskaia & Margraf, 2016), which explains, to an extent, the conflicting results across studies. Conversely, other researchers find the opposite: that increased use of social networking negatively affects young adults' abilities to interact face to face and demonstrate more depressive symptoms. On a similar note, research analyzing body image and gender in comparison to social media use also demonstrates high levels of depressive symptoms. Strubel, et al. ~~Petrie, and Pookulnagara~~ in ~~their~~ 2018 ~~study~~ defined social media as having become a form of sociocultural channel that transits body-centric information more than previous media outlets. Prior to social media and SNS, there were limited ways for individuals' body-image and self-esteem to be influenced. Social media and SNS are a newly developed, *highly*

> Comment: Pathetic fallacy error -- a study cannot posit.

> Comment: Be sure to clearly cite the researchers who found the opposite finding -- was it Strubel?

> Comment: Pathetic fallacy error -- research does not analyze.

> Comment: Good variety in sentence structure!

FIGURE 5.5. Sample Literature Review on Social Media Effects, With Instructor Edits (continued)

effective form of reinforcing hegemonic norms, particularly those that reiterate the ideal body image for both men and women. They ~~authors of this study~~ focused on the body dissatisfaction women have when they compare themselves to the ideal bodies represented consistently across social media platforms, and they ~~. The authors~~ explained that the internalization of such ideals may lead to negative emotions, such as shame, guilt, anger, and sadness among these women.

However varying or contradicting prior results may be, a consistent thread weaves across all studies: social media use and SNS use significantly impact individual mood. In order to fill the knowledge gap, I will examine the relationship between possible existing depression and the use of social media, without emphasis on specific depressive symptoms or direct analysis of number of followers. The purpose of my study is to determine if there is a relationship between depression and the use of social media.

To research the possible relationship between depression and social media use, a sample of undergraduate students will participated in an online survey. The sample will be ~~was taken from I~~introductory ~~ion to P~~psychology students ~~at Boise State University, and participants responded to compilation of several research surveys~~ from a large Western university. ~~To measure possible correlations, evaluative questions concerning the presence of depressive symptoms, as well as questions measuring the amount of media use, were presented in survey form.~~

Upon review of previous literature and research performed regarding social media, SNS, and various levels or types of depressive symptoms on individuals, I expect that this study will reproduce the most typical results found so far. The more an individual uses social media, regardless of the platform, the more that individual will experience increased levels of depression. I hypothesize, ~~first,~~ that there will be a positive correlation between depression and the use of social media. Second, I hypothesize that the platform through which an individual accesses social media or SNS will not matter; the quantifiable amount of use will be the predictor of depressive symptoms and level of depression.

> **Comment:** Pathetic fallacy error -- the study does not produce. What does this sentence add?

> **Comment:** You are predicting the null hypothesis here (which might occur). However, try to make a directional prediction.

Note. From course literature review by Izzy Riley, 2018. Copyright 2018 by Izzy Riley. Printed with permission.

FIGURE 5.6. Sample Literature Review on Social Media Effects, Final Draft (continues)

1

The Effects of Social Media Use on Depression

More than 70% of youth and young adults who use the internet use social media sites (Davila et al., 2012). Social media sites and social networking sites (SNS) range from colloquial use to professional use, as well as contemporary designs to platforms meant for professional networking. Common platforms used for studies include Instagram, Twitter, Facebook, and LinkedIn. LinkedIn is the most commonly used professional social networking site (Jones et al., 2016). Similarly, about 90% of 13- to 29-year-olds (of internet users in the U.S.) have at least one social networking site (Cavazos-Rehg et al., 2017). With the rise of social media and SNS, many researchers show interest in possible psychological problems that may also arise with the decrease of face-to-face communication, particularly in the pervasiveness of depression. With so many people in the up-and-coming generation using the internet and social media, there is bound to be significantly less interaction that is commonly attributed to a healthy lifestyle (i.e., face-to-face social interactions, outdoor time, etc.). It is necessary to understand whether there is a significant relationship between these factors and social media in order to better prepare for possible negative side effects of the rapidly growing use of social media.

Through a review of literature, I investigated the prevalence of depression, as well as the possible relationships between depression and the use of social media. According to one researcher, participants who used LinkedIn at a minimum of once per week had significantly greater chances of increased depression in comparison to the participants who did not use LinkedIn (Jones et al., 2016). Depressive symptoms appear in nonprofessional online platforms as well. For instance, another group of researchers discussed the most popular observed theme from a sample of 2,739 depression-related posts on Tumblr, and these themes were found: self-loathing, loneliness/feeling unloved, and self-harm and/or scars from self-harm (Cavazos-Rehg et al., 2017). Similarly, Twitter users expressing dissatisfaction more commonly use swear

FIGURE 5.6. Sample Literature Review on Social Media Effects, Final Draft (continued)

2

words to convey negative emotion, anger, sadness, and sexuality than other users (Yang & Srinivasan, 2016). On another note, if you search for the terms "depressed," "suicide," "self-mutilation," or "cutting," Tumblr will first send you to a screen with suggestions for seeking help (Cavazos-Rehg et al., 2017). Researchers from each of these studies emphasize the significance of depression existing across social media platforms, both professional and entertainment-based. The real question behind the compilation of all this research is to what extent depression exists, and is there an actual relationship between usage of social media and increased depressive symptoms?

Many researchers believe in the existence of a connection between depression and the use of social media; however, uncertainty still remains due to the varying topics of research in this field, which tend to lead to inconsistent or incomparable results. Researchers in this field, for example, analyzed the number of virtual friends an individual has (Sherlock & Wagstaff, 2018), as well as the types of posts that are most common within platforms (Blease, 2015), in an attempt to reduce the number of variables that might contribute to a possible relationship. Another group of researchers (Davila et al., 2012) took a more specific approach to interactions online, and examined more than merely the association between time spent on social media and depression, but also took into consideration the quality of interactions the participants engaged in. The authors of this study found that corumination, or the act of talking about problems with friends in a negative and repetitive way, can actually predict increases in depressive symptoms (Davila et al., 2012). Finding connections between quality of interactions and frequency of depressive symptoms expands the dimensions in which social media possibly affects individuals, and leads to development of more theories.

Other psychologists consider the number of followers (i.e., friends on Facebook, followers on Instagram) an individual has on social media sites. Researchers found that "...the average time spent on Instagram correlated

FIGURE 5.6. Sample Literature Review on Social Media Effects, Final Draft (continued)

3

positively with depressive symptoms, trait anxiety, social comparison orientation, physical appearance anxiety, and body image disturbance" (Sherlock & Wagstaff, 2018, p. 6). The idea that social media, in this case Instagram, affects more than just depressive symptoms, but also affects an individual's self-image and body image, leads to more questions about exactly how much of our lives can be affected by social media. Similarly, Sherlock and Wagstaff (2018) analyzed number of followers and concluded that number of followers correlated positively with depression and trait anxiety. These researchers reported a negative correlation between number of followers and self-esteem. The results are inconsistent, as the higher the number of followers actually correlates with a lower level of self-esteem. Number of followers is one way to analyze the effect of social media on its users; even so, researchers investigating the content of posts suggest that there may be other causes for depressive symptoms in users.

More experts in social media insist that content of posts, or status updates, should be a priority in identifying important components of social media or the individual that add to the intensity of depressive symptoms. Blease (2015) analyzed the specific types of status updates on Facebook. According to this research, there are three note-worthy forms of "status updates" on Facebook: updates that reveal low negative self-esteem, self-promoting updates, and self-important/narrow-minded posts. Analyzing depression from this angle becomes possible after establishing criteria behind each type of status update. Another important variable needing to be defined is the scientific term for happiness, referred to as subjective well-being, or SWB. The presence of positive emotions, the absence of negative emotions, and life satisfaction of the individual determine SWB (Yang & Srinivasan, 2016). By measuring SWB, researchers effectively evaluate the overall mood or possible prevalence of depressive symptoms. Equally as important, self-esteem can be described as "the evaluative component of the self—the degree to which one prizes, values,

FIGURE 5.6. Sample Literature Review on Social Media Effects, Final Draft (continued)

4

approves or likes oneself" (Pantic, 2014, p. 653). Types of posts, SWB, and self-esteem are all components that define how an individual sees himself or herself, and ultimately predict levels of depressive moods within social media sites.

Many researchers are interested in the relationship between social media use and depression, as well as other psychological disorders, and they have performed studies in an effort to find a correlation. Results vary drastically. Some researchers investigated the presence of increased communication or increased number of "friends," and the resulting effect on mood. Brailovskaia and Margraf (2016) posit that the absence of face-to-face interactions may make it easier to interact with other people, particularly for shy individuals, which explains to an extent the conflicting results across studies. On a similar note, researchers analyzing body image and gender in comparison to social media use also reported high levels of depressive symptoms (Strubel et al., 2018). These authors defined social media as having become a form of sociocultural channel that transits body-centric information more than previous media outlets. Prior to social media and social networking sites, there were limited ways for individuals' body-image and self-esteem to be influenced. Social media and social networking sites are a newly developed, *highly effective* form of reinforcing hegemonic norms, particularly those that reiterate the ideal body image for both men and women. The authors focused on the body dissatisfaction women have when they compare themselves to the ideal bodies represented consistently across social media platforms, and they explained that the internalization of such ideals may lead to negative emotions, such as shame, guilt, anger, and sadness among these women.

However varying or contradicting prior results may be, a consistent thread weaves across all studies: social media use significantly impacts mood. In order to fill the knowledge gap, I will examine the relationship between possible existing depression and the use of social media, without emphasis on specific depressive symptoms or direct analysis of number of followers. The purpose of

FIGURE 5.6. Sample Literature Review on Social Media Effects, Final Draft (continued)

5

my study is to determine if there is a relationship between depression and the

use of social media.

　　　　To research the possible relationship between depression and social

media use, a sample of undergraduate students will participate in an online

survey. The sample will be introductory psychology students from a large

Western university.

　　　　I expect that the more an individual uses social media, regardless of the

platform, the more that individual will experience increased levels of

depression. I hypothesize that there is a positive correlation between

depression and the use of social media. I also hypothesize that the platform

through which an individual accesses social media or social networking does not

matter; the quantifiable amount of use is the predictor of depressive symptoms

and level of depression.

Note. From course literature review by Izzy Riley, 2018. Copyright 2018 by Izzy Riley. Printed with permission.

6

Telling an Original Story Through a Research Paper

It is best to do things systematically, since we are only human, and disorder is our worst enemy.

—HESIOD, *WORKS AND DAYS*

Many of the types of scientific writing that you will be asked to complete in your psychology classes will be variations on the theme of this chapter—writing the research paper—and yes, that process is quite organized and systematic. A lab report is often a miniature version of a research paper, and a literature review could be thought of as a specialized and elongated version of an Introduction section. Because of the importance of the research paper format and the necessity of using American Psychological Association (APA) Style and format, this chapter presents real examples of research paper sections from undergraduate students (with their permission, of course), culminating in a complete paper in Chapter 7.

To make the paper preparation process more real for you, just as in Chapter 5 where I presented Izzy's original draft of an Introduction section–literature review, my edited copy, and her final draft, here I present the work of another student, Rebecca. I present sections of her research paper in the same way as I would assign them in my research methods class—first the Introduction section; then the Method, Results, and Discussion sections; then a combined assignment including the title page, abstract, references, and tables (which I call TPART—these details are covered in Chapter 7); and then the completed final draft (also presented in Chapter 7). To actively demonstrate this process for you, I present Rebecca's original draft of each assignment and my marked-up copy. Note that I have purposely kept these examples real—this is a real paper, and these are my real edits. I have not presented a perfect paper to you but a very good paper completed by a very good student. My editing marks do not identify all the possible errors in the draft, and your instructor will certainly find mistakes that I did not. The final draft that you see is not perfect, but for the assignment and in context, I deemed it distinguished work. I appreciate both Izzy and Rebecca for generously sharing their work for your benefit.

SET THE TONE: INTRODUCTION AND SAMPLE

In the previous chapter, I presented a sample Introduction section, including the literature review; however, the Introduction section is important enough that some points bear repeating. When you begin writing your Introduction, you will realize how different scientific writing is from other types of writing. Scientific writing is not as personal as a narrative, short story, or poem; rather, it is detached and objective. Even though you may be describing your personal research, you should not be personal in your writing. One of the best ways to understand this "tone" of writing is by reading examples from psychological journals. Note that better-written journal articles are easier to read; if you cannot understand the gist of an article after reading it, then I would argue that the article wasn't well written. Good science involves communication of new knowledge, and poorly written research papers and articles fail to communicate clearly.

As depicted in Chapter 5, the shape of a manuscript resembles that of an hourglass (a common analogy; see Bem, 2004). Start your Introduction broadly and become more and more narrow until you finish with specific hypotheses and predictions about the research to be conducted. How many references should be cited in your Introduction section? There is no definitive answer unless your instructor indicates this to you as part of the assignment. The literature review of a research paper is not meant to be exhaustive. The goal instead is to report on the classic, seminal work in the field and provide a current update on the present knowledge (Calderon & Austin, 2006). Using examples to help illustrate important or complicated material is an excellent way to communicate to the reader and demonstrate your thorough understanding of the concepts being presented (Bem, 2004).

A sample first draft of Rebecca's Introduction section appears in Figure 6.1. My edited version appears in Figure 6.2. (As noted earlier, the complete, final draft appears in Chapter 7.) Note that the word "Introduction" does not appear at the top of the page—instead, APA format requires that the title from page 1 be repeated at the beginning of the Introduction section.

FIGURE 6.1. Sample Introduction Section of a Research Paper, Rough Draft (continues)

Filter Bubbles: How Social Media Contributes to Social Division

American's are further apart ideologically now than at any other point in the past twenty years (Pew Research Center, 2017a) and filter bubbles may be to blame (Pariser, 2011). Pew Research Center reported 32% of U.S. citizens had both liberal and conservative views on social issues compared to 49% in 1994 (2017a). With social media at the forefront of personal broadcasting, polarizing social opinions can be viewed online. Out of the U.S. adults who use the internet, 79% use Facebook (Pew Research Center, 2016). With social media being so prevalent in society, there could be a correlation between social media and the increase in political division. The theory of the filter bubble could explain how social media and political division impact one another (Pariser, 2011). In 2011, Eli Pariser explained how filter bubbles are created by algorithms that personalize what people see online, meaning that two people could search the same thing and receive differing results. This could lead to each person developing a personalized filter bubble that keeps new or different information out (Pariser, 2011). Eli Pariser also expressed that filter bubbles are present on social media sites with user filtration options being available — unfollowing, unfriending, blocking.

Researchers found that social media is used more often as social surveillance instead of communication and interaction (Hall, 2016). Social surveillance means that less time is spent commenting and messaging, more time is spent scrolling and viewing what people have posted (Hall, 2016). It is not uncommon for social media users to obtain news on social media sites (Pew Research Center, 2017b). After a survey study, researchers found that 74.8% of survey respondents experienced political disagreement on social media (Yang, Barnidge, & Rojas, 2016). There is evidence that neither social media engagement level nor political disagreement are significantly related to social media users filtering out disagreement from the respective platform (Yang, et al., 2016). There is a strong overlap in social networks for online and offline

FIGURE 6.1. Sample Introduction Section of a Research Paper, Rough Draft (continued)

relationships (Sutcliffe, Binder, & Dunbar, 2018), suggesting that people could be equally selective about who they interact with offline and online. Researchers have found that enjoyment is what drives social media users to continue using social media sites, social media users are likely to spend more time on social media if they enjoy the content (Li, Li, Gan, Liu, Tan, & Deng, 2018). Zilberstein states that there is little significant evidence that technology weakens social bonds and keeps new ideas from people (2015). Trends occur throughout history with and without social media, proposing that technology performs as a medium for expressing ideas already present in society (Zilberstein, 2015). However, users constructing an online experience filled with only information that is familiar could lead to intellectual isolation (Pariser, 2011).

Does the presence of personalized filter bubbles on social media aid in social division? The purpose of my study is to determine if social media users create filter bubbles that promote intellectual isolation and social division.

A survey was administered to a section of Introduction to Psychology students at Boise State University. I examined whether or not social media users filter out people and information they disagree with by hiding, unfollowing, unfriending, and blocking. Then, I determined if those who filter more often have more polarizing opinions on social issues.

I hypothesize that social media users create highly selective filter bubbles. I hypothesize that the more selective an individual is with social media filtration, the more polarizing their opinions will be on social issues.

Note. From course research paper by Rebecca Cuthbertson, 2018. Copyright 2018 by Rebecca Cuthbertson. Adapted with permission.

FIGURE 6.2. Sample Introduction Section of a Research Paper, With Instructor Edits (continues)

Filter Bubbles: How Social Media Contributes to Social Division

American's are further apart ideologically now than at any other point in the past twenty years (Pew Research Center, 2017a) and filter bubbles may be to blame (Pariser, 2011). Pew Research Center (2017a) reported that 32% of U.S. citizens had both liberal and conservative views on social issues compared to 49% in 1994 (2017a). With social media at the forefront of personal broadcasting, polarizing social opinions can be viewed online. Out of the U.S. adults who use the internetInternet, 79% use Facebook (Pew Research Center, 2016). With social media being so prevalent in society, there could be a correlation relationship between social media and the increase in political division. The theory of the filter bubble could explain how social media and political division impact one another (Pariser, 2011). In 2011, Eli Pariser explained how filter bubbles are created by algorithms that personalize what people see online, meaning that two people could search the same thing and receive differing results. This could lead to each person developing a personalized filter bubble that keeps new or different information out (Pariser, 2011). Eli Pariser also expressed that filter bubbles are present on social media sites with user filtration options being available—unfollowing, unfriending, blocking.

Researchers found that social media is used more often as social surveillance instead of communication and interaction (Hall, 2016). Social surveillance means that less time is spent commenting and messaging, more time is spent scrolling and viewing what people have posted (Hall, 2016). It is not uncommon for social media users to obtain news on social media sites (Pew Research Center, 2017b). After a survey study, researchers found that 74.8% of survey respondents experienced political disagreement on social media (Yang, et al.Barnidge, & Rojas, 2016). There is evidence that neither social media engagement level nor political disagreement are significantly related to social media users filtering out disagreement from the respective platform (Yang, et al., 2016). There is a strong overlap in social networks for online and offline relationships (Sutcliffe, Binder, & Dunbar et al., 2018), suggesting that people could be equally selective about who they interact with offline and online. Researchers have found that enjoyment is what drives social media users to continue using social media sites, social media users are likely to spend more time on social media if they enjoy the content (Li, Li, Gan, Liu, Tan, & Deng et al.,

Comment: In the top margin, the page number is missing; it should be flush with the right margin.

Comment: Capitalization rules for technology terms have been updated in the seventh edition of the *Publication Manual* (see p. 162, Section 6.11) and "internet" is now lowercase, so original is correct.

Comment: Avoid using the word "thing" – it's too vague.

Comment: Do not use first names.

Comment: This is a well-written opening section.

Comment: Per the seventh edition of the *Publication Manual*, when citing a work with three or more authors, include only the first author name followed by "et al." in every citation (see p. 266, Section 8.17).

FIGURE 6.2. Sample Introduction Section of a Research Paper, With Instructor Edits (continued)

2018). Zilberstein (2015) ~~states~~ stated that there is little significant evidence that technology weakens social bonds and keeps new ideas from people ~~(2015)~~. Trends occur throughout history with and without social media, proposing that technology performs as a medium for expressing ideas already present in society (Zilberstein, 2015). However, users constructing an online experience filled with only information that is familiar could lead to intellectual isolation (Pariser, 2011).

> **Comment:** With two citations in a row from the same source, you only need to provide the second citation.

    Does the presence of personalized filter bubbles on social media aid in social division? The purpose of my study is to determine if social media users create filter bubbles that promote intellectual isolation and social division.

> **Comment:** You've provided many citations in this paragraph, but now, try to tie them all together here at the end of the paragraph. What is the overall meaning? Why did you select these citations, to make what point?

    A~~n online~~ survey was administered to ~~a~~ section~~s~~ of ~~i~~Introductor~~y~~~~ion to~~ p~~P~~sychology ~~students~~ at a large Western ~~Boise State U~~university. I examined whether or not social media users filter out people and information they disagree with by hiding, unfollowing, unfriending, and blocking. Then, I determined if those who filter more often have more polarizing opinions on social issues.

> **Comment:** It really would have been much better to describe the gap/hole in the research, and why it is necessary for your research to resolve the conflict and fill the gap.

    I hypothesize that social media users create highly selective filter bubbles. I hypothesize that the more selective an individual is with social media filtration, the more polarizing their opinions will be on social issues.

> **Comment:** Overall, this is very well-written. There are just some spots where there should have been more (the gap/hole/conflict to be resolved).

Note. From course research paper by Rebecca Cuthbertson, 2018. Copyright 2018 by Rebecca Cuthbertson. Adapted with permission.

TOTAL TRANSPARENCY: METHOD SECTION AND SAMPLE

The Method section tells the reader exactly how the study was conducted. You describe your participants, materials, and procedure in three separate subsections of the Method section. Although the Method section may appear to be dry reading, it is important. The Method section provides a blueprint for other researchers, especially if they want to replicate (repeat) your study. In psychology and other sciences, we don't keep secrets. We tell the world exactly how we conducted our study, down to the nitty-gritty details. Your study should be an open book, and your Method section should provide enough detail that if another researcher wanted to replicate your study, they would be able to do so. This open, objective feature—the transparency of one's method—is an important component of science not only because it allows researchers to build on one another's work, but also because this method builds trust. Revealing all the details means that the researcher has nothing to hide. This invites replication and is a characteristic of good science.

Participants

Tell the reader who participated in your study. In this section, you need to report (a) who took part in the study, (b) how many participants there were, (c) how the participants were selected, and (d) any pertinent demographic characteristics. Typically, demographic variables include sex (gender), age, and race or ethnicity. (Note: If you are reporting the mean [average] age, remember that you must also report its corresponding standard deviation. In APA format, every measure of central tendency must be accompanied by a measure of variability.) Report here any demographic variables that are related to the hypotheses you are testing. For example, if you were conducting a study on political attitudes about some aspect of governmental functioning, it might be an important demographic to report the breakdown of Republican, Democrat, and Independent participants.

Materials (or Apparatus)

Describe all the materials used to conduct the study. Essentially, this is a listing of the equipment needed to conduct the study. Did you use a computer to present stimulus items on the screen? Did you video record participants and later analyze their behavior? Did you develop a survey and then administer it to participants? Were you involved in any pilot testing before working with actual participants? Describe the materials you used in enough detail that someone else would be able to recreate them, or find your sources and obtain them. If you developed original survey questions, include them in a table or appendix. If you used a specialized computer program, be sure to give the details so that someone else would be able to obtain and use a similar program. The term *apparatus* refers to the specialized equipment that a study may have required. Not every Method section will have an Apparatus section.

Procedure

This portion of your Method section describes how the study was completed from the first step to the last step. Provide enough information about the procedure so that another researcher could replicate the study. This might include the instructions given to participants if the instructions are an important part of the independent variable manipulation in your study. Describe how participants were assigned to groups or subgroups, addressing issues such as randomization or counterbalancing as appropriate. If you developed a new technique, describe it in enough detail that others could replicate it. Be sure to include any debriefing accounts if that was part of your research study.

In my research methods course, Rebecca developed a small set of survey questions that were added to a larger set from the entire class. Given that this is a survey study, the details are fairly straightforward. I present her first rough draft of the Method section in Figure 6.3 and my marked-up version in Figure 6.4.

WHAT HAPPENED, BUT NOT WHY: RESULTS SECTION AND SAMPLE

The major purpose of the Results section is to report the findings of your research. If you are going to include a table or figure, it is usually referred to somewhere in the Results section. In my research methods course, every hypothesis mentioned at the end of the Introduction section must be specifically addressed in the Results section, regardless of whether the hypothesis was supported or not. Follow APA format for the reporting of descriptive and inferential statistics. For instance, in descriptive statistics, every time you report a mean you need to report its corresponding standard deviation, thus providing a measure of central tendency and a measure of variability, respectively. When using inferential statistics, you need to italicize the symbol representing the statistic (e.g., r, t, or F) and include a p-value statement toward the end of your sentence (be sure to check with your instructor to see if they want a measure of effect size included with your statistical results). Begin your Results section with the outcome that is most important to your research (Salovey, 2000). I tell my students to start with the "big bang" of the findings and report the most important finding first.

Bem (2004) suggested the following sequence for the presentation of information in the Results section:

1. Verify that your study was successful in setting up the conditions needed to adequately test your hypothesis (i.e., that nothing major went wrong in the conduct of the study).

2. Describe your overall approach to data analysis, including the methodology used to obtain your dependent variable measurements.

FIGURE 6.3. Sample Method Section of a Research Paper, Rough Draft

Method

Participants

      This study was conducted with XXX participants from introductory psychology sections at a large Western university. Women comprised XX% of participants, men XX%. Ages ranged from XX to XX, with the mean age of XX.XX years (*SD* = X.XX). Participants voluntarily completed a survey and were rewarded course credit.

Materials

      Survey items were developed to measure the presence of filtered social media use and participant opinion polarization. A pilot test was conducted with students in a research methods class. For the list of survey items, refer to Table 1.

Procedure

      Participants were self-selected via Sona Systems and completed the survey individually online through Qualtrics. The allotted time to complete the survey was 60 minutes, with the average completion time being XX.XX minutes (*SD* = X.XX). Upon completion, participants were thanked but not debriefed. Results from each survey were compiled for analysis.

Note. From course research paper by Rebecca Cuthbertson, 2018. Copyright 2018 by Rebecca Cuthbertson. Adapted with permission.

FIGURE 6.4. Sample Method Section of a Research Paper, With Instructor Edits

Method

Participants

      This study was conducted with XXX participants from introductory psychology sections at a large Western university. ~~Females~~Women comprised XX% of participants, ~~males~~men XX%. Ages ranged from XX to XX, with the mean age of XX.XX (*SD* ⬛ X.XX). Participants voluntarily completed a survey and were rewarded course credit.

> **Comment:** The seventh edition of the *Publication Manual* recommends using "male" and "female" as adjectives, not nouns. Use specific nouns to refer to groups of people (women, men) unless the age range is broad or ambiguous.

Materials

      I developed sSurvey items ~~were developed~~ to measure the presence of filtered social media use and participant opinion polarization. A pilot test was conducted with students in a research methods class. For the list of survey items, refer to Table 1.

> **Comment:** Treat the equal sign like a word, with a space on both sides.

Procedure

      Participants were self-selected via Sona Systems and completed the survey individually online through Qualtrics. The allotted time to complete the survey was 60 ~~minutes~~, with the average completion time being XX.XX ~~minutes~~ (*SD* ⬛ X.XX). Upon completion, participants were thanked but not debriefed. ~~Results from each survey were compiled for analysis.~~

Note. From course research paper by Rebecca Cuthbertson, 2018. Copyright 2018 by Rebecca Cuthbertson. Adapted with permission.

3. Provide a brief reminder of the main conceptual question or hypothesis, and a reminder about the basic tests performed and behaviors measured. Sometimes readers will read parts of a research paper (or journal article) out of order. The reminders save the readers from having to look for the context to interpret the section they are reading.

4. Answer your hypotheses as clearly and unequivocally as you can, first using words, then presenting your statistical evidence in numbers in APA format.

5. After addressing the major hypotheses of the study, address other findings or surprises that emerged. Use the same format: describe what happened clearly, in words, then numbers.

6. You may want to organize your Results section into logical subsections if that will help the reader follow the story. Be sure to use the proper APA Style headings as signposts, just as you did with the Participants, Materials, and Procedure subsections of the Method section.

7. As you move from paragraph to paragraph in the Results section, try to provide smooth transitions between paragraphs, emphasizing the logical flow of your hypothesis testing and the outcomes of your research.

Plonsky (2006) offered additional advice on what *not* to do in a Results section:

- Do not discuss the implications of the results in the Results section; that is saved for the Discussion section.

- Do not discuss the alpha level or the null hypothesis because most readers in the scientific community will already understand these assumptions.

- Do not organize subsections of your Results section by type of analysis (all the *t* tests in one paragraph, all the correlations in the next); instead, organize subsections by variable to be studied or hypothesis to be tested.

- Do not present the raw data collected unless that is part of your instructor's assignment.

- Do not use the word "proved" because in science the researcher never proves anything; they only disprove competing theories and hypotheses until one logical explanation is left—which, hopefully, is the working hypothesis. But that is not necessarily the case.

If you are wondering why Rebecca's descriptive statistics section is relatively short, it is because she was following the guidelines of her instructor. Figure 6.5 presents her rough draft; Figure 6.6 presents my marked-up copy.

FIGURE 6.5. Sample Results Section of a Research Paper, Rough Draft (continues)

1

Results

I hypothesized that social media users create filter bubbles. The key question of interest will be "I will hide, unfriend, or unfollow people on social media for expressing opinions that are different than mine," which was measured on a scale from 1 = *strongly disagree* to 5 = *strongly agree*. The hypothesis was tested by comparing the key question to the items "I often express my social/political opinions on social media" and "my opinions on controversial topics can change due to conversations on social media," both were measured on a scale from 1 = *strongly disagree* to 5 = *strongly agree*. There is a statistically significant relationship between answers to the key item and answers to the item "I often express my social/political opinions on social media," $r(157) = .26$, $p = .001$. There is a statistically significant relationship between responses to the key item and responses to the item "my opinions on controversial topics can change due to conversations on social media," $r(157) = .22$, $p = .005$.

I hypothesized that individuals who hide, unfollow, or unfriend people on social media for expressing different opinions would have more polarizing responses to political questions. The key item is "I will hide, unfriend, or unfollow people on social media for expressing opinions that are different than mine," measured on a scale from 1 = *strongly disagree* to 5 = *strongly agree*. The two political items are "politics should not be influenced by religion" and "marijuana should be legalized," both measured on a scale from 1 = *strongly disagree* to 5 = *strongly agree*. To test the hypothesis, key item responses were compared to the responses on the political items. There is not a statistically significant relationship between responses to the key item and responses to the item "politics should not be influenced by religion," $r(157) = -.03$, $p = .678$. There is not a statistically significant relationship between the key item responses and "marijuana should be legalized," $r(157) = -.02$, $p = .795$.

The item "Politically, I identify as" had the following response options; 1 = *Republican*, 2 = *Democrat*, 3 = *Independent*. Political identification was then compared to the item "I often express my

FIGURE 6.5. Sample Results Section of a Research Paper, Rough Draft (continued)

2

social/political opinions on social media," which was measured on a scale from 1 = *strongly disagree* to 5 = *strongly agree*. There is a statistically significant difference between individuals who identified as Republican (M = 2.00, SD = 1.12), Democrat (M = 2.08, SD = 1.05), or Independent (M = 1.46, SD = 0.79) and their response to the item "I often express my social/political opinions on social media," $F(2,146)$ = 4.67, p = .011.

Individuals identified their gender with the following response options: 1 = *male*, 2 = *female*, and 3 = *other*. Gender was then compared to the item "I will hide, unfriend, or unfollow people on social media for expressing opinions that are different than mine," which was measured on a scale from 1 = *strongly disagree* to 5 = *strongly agree*. There is a statistically significant difference between males (M = 1.74, SD = 0.85) and females (M = 2.13, SD = 0.93) on responses to the item "I will hide, unfriend, or unfollow people on social media for expressing opinions that are different than mine," $F(1,147)$ = 5.76, p = .018.

Note. From course research paper by Rebecca Cuthbertson, 2018. Copyright 2018 by Rebecca Cuthbertson. Adapted with permission.

FIGURE 6.6. Sample Results Section of a Research Paper, With Instructor Edits (continues)

1

Results

> **Formatted:** Space After: 0 pt

I hypothesized that social media users create filter bubbles. The key question of interest will be "I will hide, unfriend, or unfollow people on social media for expressing opinions that are different than mine," which was measured on a scale from 1 = *strongly disagree* to 5 = *strongly agree*. The hypothesis was tested by comparing the key question to the items "I often express my social/political opinions on social media" and "my opinions on controversial topics can change due to conversations on social media," both were measured on a scale from 1 = *strongly disagree* to 5 = *strongly agree*. There is a statistically significant relationship between answers to the key item and answers to the item "I often express my social/political opinions on social media," $r(157) = .26$, $p = .001$. There is a statistically significant relationship between responses to the key item and responses to the item "my opinions on controversial topics can change due to conversations on social media," $r(157) = .22$, $p = .005$.

I hypothesized that individuals who hide, unfollow, or unfriend people on social media for expressing different opinions would have more polarizing responses to political questions. The key item is "I will hide, unfriend, or unfollow people on social media for expressing opinions that are different than mine," measured on a scale from 1 = *strongly disagree* to 5 = *strongly agree*. The two political items are "politics should not be influenced by religion" and "marijuana should be legalized," both measured on a scale from 1 = *strongly disagree* to 5 = *strongly agree*. To test the hypothesis, key item responses were compared to the responses on the political items. There is not a statistically significant relationship between responses to the key item and responses to the item "politics should not be influenced by religion," $r(157) = -.03$, $p = .678$. There is not a statistically significant relationship between the key item responses and "marijuana should be legalized," $r(157) = -.02$, $p = .795$.

> **Comment:** No extra spaces after paragraphs (remove all).

> **Comment:** Treat an equal sign like a word, and place a space on both sides of the sign.

The item "Politically, I identify as" had the following response options; 1 = *Republican*, 2 = *Democrat*, 3 = *Independent*. Political identification was then compared to the item "I often express my

FIGURE 6.6. Sample Results Section of a Research Paper, With Instructor Edits (continued)

2

social/political opinions on social media," which was measured on a scale from 1 = *strongly disagree* to 5 = *strongly agree*. There is a statistically significant difference between individuals who identified as Republican (M = 2.00, SD = 1.12), Democrat (M = 2.08, SD = 1.05), or Independent (M = 1.46, SD = 0.79) and their response to the item "I often express my social/political opinions on social media," $F(2,146)$ = 4.67, p = .011.

Individuals identified their gender with the following response options: 1 = *male*, 2 = *female*, and 3 = *other*. Gender was then compared to the item "I will hide, unfriend, or unfollow people on social media for expressing opinions that are different than mine," which was measured on a scale from 1 = *strongly disagree* to 5 = *strongly agree*. There is a statistically significant difference between males (M = 1.74, SD = 0.85) and females (M = 2.13, SD = 0.93) on responses to the item "I will hide, unfriend, or unfollow people on social media for expressing opinions that are different than mine," $F(1,147)$ = 5.76, p = .018.

Comment: You did an outstanding job on this Results section!

Note. From course research paper by Rebecca Cuthbertson, 2018. Copyright 2018 by Rebecca Cuthbertson. Adapted with permission.

EXPLAIN AND QUESTION AGAIN: DISCUSSION SECTION AND SAMPLE

In the Discussion section, you finally get the chance to interpret all the results that were presented in the Results section. Here is where you have the opportunity to finish telling the story that you began in the Introduction section. What happened? What worked, and what did not work? What will the reader be able to conclude from your study? The Discussion section starts out very specific—what happened in the study—and gets broader with generalizations and conclusions. Essentially, the Discussion section is the bottom of the hourglass—it starts out narrow with answers to your specific hypotheses and then widens, ending with the implications of your study for future researchers.

As with the Introduction section, I provide my students with a rubric that outlines my expectations (especially in regard to grading). Be sure to ask your instructor before every writing assignment if there is a rubric you can review. Not every item included in the list of expectations will be its own paragraph in the resulting Discussion section, and some items may require more than one paragraph. Remember, after you've read more psychology journal articles and written more psychology research papers, you'll feel comfortable moving away from the template to your own style that complies with APA format. Not every Discussion section I have written includes the following six points, but this template is a good start.

- Begin your Discussion with the most important finding of the study—what I call the "big bang." What happened? Did you find anything that was unexpected, unusual, fascinating, interesting, unique, or counterintuitive? The first paragraph of your Discussion section should have the "take-home" message—if the reader is to remember only one piece of information from this study, what is it? The major premise of your study should be described here—whether something turned out the way you expected or didn't turn out the way you expected.

- Briefly restate the hypotheses from the end of your Introduction section and discuss whether they were supported on the basis of the study's outcomes. Be specific (e.g., "Significant gender differences were found for the questions regarding X, X, and X. In all cases, men were more favorable toward these questions than women. This means that. . . ."). Thus, all hypotheses, whether supported or not, are addressed somewhere in the Discussion section. Place your study in the context of the studies that have preceded yours. This means revisiting some of the literature you cited in the Introduction section and including it here.

- Did you fill that knowledge gap or hole that you identified early on? Although you may have answered one question, perhaps your study raised three new ones (this is typical in psychological research—it's called job security!). If your study contradicts previous research, then you need to speculate about why that happened—for example, perhaps it was a different subject population or the methodologies were dramatically different. Cite studies in this part of the Discussion section to show that you see the how your particular research fits into the bigger picture.

- Now generalize a bit about the results of your study. Look beyond, to a broader context than just those tested. Here you get to speculate on the greater impact of your research, but be sure to label speculation as such. What do the results of your study mean? In other words, could the results of your study be useful in setting policies about human behavior? How might they be interpreted in a broader context beyond the sample you studied?

- Present the limitations of your study, but don't be too hard on yourself—no study has ever been conducted perfectly. In general, write the Discussion section as if everything was measured perfectly, but also present what went wrong—what do you wish you had done differently? Did you have enough participants to adequately test your hypotheses? What should be the next study? Make some suggestions regarding the direction of future research in this field. What do you suggest be done next?

- Conclude your Discussion section with a brief paragraph that (a) restates your take-home message (the big bang), (b) reiterates the importance of your study in filling an existing knowledge gap in the literature, and (c) emphasizes the general importance of your topic. This helps justify to the reader the worthiness of your work, and it provides a nice broad completion to the bottom of the hourglass. As Bem (2004) put it, "End with a bang, not a whimper" (p. 203).

Rebecca's first draft of her Discussion section is included in Figure 6.7; my editorial marks are presented in Figure 6.8.

The four sections presented in this chapter—Introduction, Method, Results, and Discussion—constitute the bulk of the research paper. However, there are still several important details to address before your paper is complete. Finishing those final details with style is the topic of the next chapter.

FIGURE 6.7. Sample Discussion Section of a Research Paper, Rough Draft (continues)

1

Discussion

The purpose of my study is to assess whether social media users contribute to the construction of filter bubbles on social media. Social media users who express their social and political opinions on social media are more likely to hide, unfriend, or unfollow users who have different political opinions. However, user filtration on social media does not have a significant relationship with polarizing political opinions.

I hypothesized that social media users create filter bubbles. In support of this hypothesis, a significant relationship was found between individuals who express political opinions on social media and their tendency to filter those who hold opposing views. This means that those who express their opinion on social media are more likely to hide, unfriend, and unfollow people who disagree or express opposing opinions. This aligns well with my hypothesis. A significant relationship was found between filtering out opposing views on social media and an individual's capacity to change their opinion due to conversations on social media. This means that individuals who reported filtering out opposing views on social media also reported that their opinions on controversial issues can change due to conversations on social media. This result seems counterintuitive. My assumption is that those who filter out opposing opinions are less likely to change their opinions on controversial topics. This unexpected result could be due to participants being reluctant to admit to having unyielding opinions. Another possibility is that individuals who reported using filtration methods encounter more political conversations on social media than individuals who do not use filtration. If an individual is exposed to more political conversation, they could be more likely to change their views while also being more prone to use filtration methods.

I hypothesized that individuals who hide, unfollow, or unfriend people on social media for expressing different opinions would have more polarizing political opinions. There was not a significant relationship between social media filtration and polarizing opinions. This means that the level of agreement an

FIGURE 6.7. Sample Discussion Section of a Research Paper, Rough Draft (continued)

2

individual has on social or political issues is not impacted by whether or not they filter out opposing viewpoints.

With the political divide widening (Pew Research Center, 2017a) and social media becoming more prevalent (Pew Research Center, 2016), some individuals have questioned whether there is a relationship between the two. Eli Pariser expressed that filter bubbles are present on social media sites with user filtration options being available — unfollowing, unfriending, blocking (2011). Researchers found that 74.8% of survey respondents experienced political disagreement on social media (Yang, Barnidge, & Rojas, 2016). Researchers have suggested that there is a strong overlap in social networks for online and offline relationships (Sutcliffe, Binder, & Dunbar, 2018). Research on filter bubbles is limited, there is little evidence that suggests social media users contribute to filter bubbles. In my study, a significant relationship was found between expressing political opinions on social media and filtering differing opinions. This aligns with the thoughts of Eli Pariser, social media users could be contributing to the construction of filter bubbles when confronted with differing beliefs online (2011). Future study items that would help clarify the presence and construction of filter bubbles include: how social media users decide who they are going to interact with online, how often individuals encounter political posts on social media, and how often individuals engage with people offline that have differing social or political views.

Social media users who express their social and political opinions are more likely to hide, unfriend, or unfollow users who have different political opinions. It is important to acknowledge this relationship and address how this could impact social division. Political division has been getting worse and filtering out opposing opinions online could be hindering the progression toward common ground. While I found a relationship between expressing opinions and social media filtration due to disagreement, there was an overwhelming amount of responses from individuals indicating they do not express their ideas online or use filtration methods. When asked "I often express my social/political opinion on social media," 76.3% of participants

FIGURE 6.7. Sample Discussion Section of a Research Paper, Rough Draft (continued)

3

reported either disagree or strongly disagree. When asked "I will hide, unfriend, or unfollow people on social media for expressing opinions that are different than mine," 70.9% of participants reported either disagree or strongly disagree. These responses were surprising, but do not indicate that these social media users are not in a filter bubble. I assume that there is a high level of disagreement because these individuals do not feel the need to express their opinions or use filtration methods on social media. I speculate that these individuals do not feel the need to express their opinions or filter information because they are already surrounded by like-minded people on social media. I theorize that the foundation of filter bubbles may be formed offline, then transferred to an online medium and fine-tuned with social media filtration options. In future research, a more in-depth look at the development of social networks and their translation to an online medium could provide further understanding of filter bubbles, online interaction, and social division.

There were limitations on the number of survey items I was able to ask, there are also corrections I would make to existing survey items. First, I was only able to ask six questions. Under this constraint, the survey items should have been restricted to only questions pertaining to social media filtration – rather than involve polarizing opinions. If the survey items involving polarizing opinions were discarded, this would make room for more questions establishing social media use and filtration. In regard to the current survey items I would change, frequency scales – rather than agreement scales – would have been a better approach for measuring expression of political opinions, the use of social media filters, and whether conversations on social media can change political opinions.

Social media users who express their social and political opinions on social media are more likely to hide, unfriend, or unfollow users who have different political opinions. This aligns with the theory that social media users aid in the construction of filter bubbles. If further research on filter bubbles were to be conducted, counteracting social division could be possible and progressive conversations could happen.

FIGURE 6.8. Sample Discussion Section of a Research Paper, With Instructor Edits (continues)

1

Discussion

The purpose of my study is to assess whether social media users contribute to the construction of filter bubbles on social media. Social media users who express their social and political opinions on social media are more likely to hide, unfriend, or unfollow users who have different political opinions. However, user filtration on social media does not have a significant relationship with polarizing political opinions.

I hypothesized that social media users create filter bubbles. In support of this hypothesis, a significant relationship was found between individuals who express political opinions on social media and their tendency to filter those who hold opposing views. This means that those who express their opinion on social   **Comment:** Good

media are more likely to hide, unfriend, and unfollow people who disagree or express opposing opinions. This aligns well with my hypothesis. A significant relationship was found between filtering out opposing views on social media and an individual's capacity to change their opinion due to conversations on social media. This means that individuals who reported filtering out opposing views on social media also reported that their opinions on controversial issues can change due to conversations on social media. This result seems counterintuitive. My assumption is that those who filter out opposing opinions are less likely to change their opinions on controversial topics. This unexpected result could be due to participants being reluctant to admit to having unyielding opinions. Another possibility is that individuals who reported using filtration methods encounter more political conversations on social media than individuals who do not use filtration. If an individual is exposed to more political conversation, they could be more likely to change their views while also being more prone to use filtration methods.

I hypothesized that individuals who hide, unfollow, or unfriend people on social media for expressing different opinions would have more polarizing political opinions. There was not a significant relationship between social media filtration and polarizing opinions. This means that the level of agreement an individual has on social or political issues is not impacted by whether or not they filter out opposing viewpoints.

With the political divide widening (Pew Research Center, 2017a) and social media becoming more prevalent (Pew Research Center, 2016), some

FIGURE 6.8. Sample Discussion Section of a Research Paper, With Instructor Edits (continued)

2

individuals have questioned whether there is a relationship between the two. ~~Eli~~ Pariser (2011) expressed that filter bubbles are present on social media sites with user filtration options being available — unfollowing, unfriending, blocking ~~(2011)~~. Researchers found that 74.8% of survey respondents experienced political disagreement on social media (Yang, ~~Barnidge, & Rojas~~et al., 2016).

> **Comment:** Since you cited these authors originally in your introduction, do not repeat all three author names here, but just use (Yang et al., 2016).
>
> The same applies for Sutcliffe on the next line.

Researchers have suggested that there is a strong overlap in social networks for online and offline relationships (Sutcliffe, ~~Binder, & Dunbar~~ et al., 2018). Research on filter bubbles is limited, there is little evidence that suggests social media users contribute to filter bubbles. In my study, a significant relationship was found between expressing political opinions on social media and filtering differing opinions. This aligns with the thoughts of ~~Eli~~ Pariser (2011), social

> **Comment:** Do not use first names.

media users could be contributing to the construction of filter bubbles when confronted with differing beliefs online ~~(2011)~~. Future study items that would

> **Comment:** APA Style per seventh edition is to include the year immediately after the author name in a narrative citation.

help clarify the presence and construction of filter bubbles include: how social media users decide who they are going to interact with online, how often individuals encounter political posts on social media, and how often individuals engage with people offline that have differing social or political views.

    Social media users who express their social and political opinions are more likely to hide, unfriend, or unfollow users who have different political opinions. It is important to acknowledge this relationship and address how this could impact social division. Political division has been getting worse and filtering out opposing opinions online could be hindering the progression toward common ground. ~~While~~ Although I found a relationship between expressing opinions and social media filtration due to disagreement, there was an overwhelming amount of responses from individuals indicating they do not express their ideas online or use filtration methods. When asked "I often express my social/political opinion on social media," 76.3% of participants reported either disagree or strongly disagree. When asked "I will hide, unfriend, or unfollow people on social media for expressing opinions that are different than mine," 70.9% of participants reported either disagree or strongly disagree. These responses were surprising, but do not indicate that these social media users are not in a filter bubble. I assume that there is a high level of disagreement because these individuals do not feel the need to express their opinions or use filtration methods on social media. I speculate that these

FIGURE 6.8. Sample Discussion Section of a Research Paper, With Instructor Edits (continued)

3

individuals do not feel the need to express their opinions or filter information because they are already surrounded by like-minded people on social media. I theorize that the foundation of filter bubbles may be formed offline, then   **Comment:** Good

transferred to an online medium and fine-tuned with social media filtration options. In future research, a more in-depth look at the development of social networks and their translation to an online medium could provide further understanding of filter bubbles, online interaction, and social division.

There were limitations on the number of survey items I was able to ask, there are also corrections I would make to existing survey items. First, I was only able to ask six questions. Under this constraint, the survey items should have been restricted to only questions pertaining to social media filtration – rather than involve polarizing opinions. If the survey items involving polarizing opinions were discarded, this would make room for more questions establishing social media use and filtration. In regard to the current survey items I would change, frequency scales – rather than agreement scales – would have been a better approach for measuring expression of political opinions, the use of social media filters, and whether conversations on social media can change political opinions.

Social media users who express their social and political opinions on social media are more likely to hide, unfriend, or unfollow users who have different political opinions. This aligns with the theory that social media users aid in the construction of filter bubbles. If further research on filter bubbles were to be conducted, counteracting social division could be possible and progressive conversations could happen.

Note. From course research paper by Rebecca Cuthbertson, 2018. Copyright 2018 by Rebecca Cuthbertson. Adapted with permission.

7

The Rest of the Story

Title, Abstract, References, and Tables

Perhaps the most valuable result of all that education is the ability to make yourself do the thing you have to do, when it ought to be done, whether you like it or not.

—THOMAS HUXLEY, *TECHNICAL EDUCATION*

In the previous chapter, I covered the sections that comprise the bulk of your research paper; however, there are still details to finish before your research paper is complete. Although the title page will be page 1 and the abstract will be page 2, I instruct students to wait until the four main sections of the paper (Introduction, Method, Results, and Discussion) are in draft form before starting on these remaining sections. Why? You cannot write an abstract of your study if your study is not complete. Each of these four parts of the manuscript (title page, abstract, references, and tables) are important and have explicit requirements in American Psychological Association (APA) Style (2020). Next you'll find brief descriptions of each part, with details and examples of how each is prepared. Because I have my students do these parts after writing their Discussion section, I group them together and call the assignment TPART: (t)itle (p)age, (a)bstract, (r)eferences, and (t)ables.

TITLES AND ABSTRACTS FOR POSTERITY'S SAKE

Remember that every page is numbered, including the title page. The page numbering appears inside the 1-in. margin, flush right. APA Style does not impose limitations on title length, but authors are encouraged to keep their titles focused and succinct. If you have trouble creating a title for your research paper, here is a generic version of a title: "The Effects of the Independent Variable on the Dependent Variable"—just substitute in your independent and dependent variables. Other typical forms of the title may start with "A Study of . . . ," "An Investigation of . . . ," or "An Experiment on . . ." (Sternberg, 2000).

The title you select is more important than you might think, especially if you continue to write in psychology and writing becomes part of your career. The title is important for capturing the reader's attention, for indexing the article in databases, and for helping to form first impressions (Sternberg, 2000). Sternberg provided a great example of how a title can provide a positive first impression. A seminal article in cognitive psychology and human memory research is George Miller's (1956) "The Magic Number Seven, Plus or Minus Two: Some Limits on Our Capacity to Process Information." Imagine if the title had been "Limitations on Information-Processing Capacity: A Review of the Literature" (Sternberg, 2000, p. 38).

The seventh edition of the APA *Publication Manual* (2020) instructs student authors to include affiliation, name of the course, name of the instructor, and assignment due date on the title page. You might want to check with your instructor to make sure they want all of that included and whether they want any additional information included. Also note that the title page is double-spaced—you'll see this in the example that follows and also in the very helpful sample paper starting on page 61 of the *Publication Manual* (APA, 2020).

For new writers of research papers, I think the abstract can be the most difficult section to write. You have just completed this study demonstrating your comprehension and knowledge of a complex behavioral phenomenon, and now you are asked to condense this massive amount of work into one paragraph that is typically between 150 and 250 words. Writing a coherent abstract is truly an art form, in my opinion. The best way to get a sense of what abstracts should contain is to read them in journal articles and refer to other examples, such as the one in the sample paper here. In the publication world, the abstract is very important because it becomes part of a database record, which means that it is a key resource for researchers when identifying which articles might be relevant to their work. Prospective readers will read your title first, and then, if it sounds interesting, the abstract second (Sternberg, 2000). However, your instructor will be reading your work no matter what.

The abstract starts at the top of page 2 in the manuscript, with the word "Abstract" centered and in boldface on the first line. The abstract is one paragraph long, not indented, and as per APA format, typically ranges between 150 to 250 words. Use the word-count feature of your word-processing program to determine the number of words in your abstract. Will your instructor actually count the words? Probably not, but they will have a good sense of whether the abstract is too long just by looking at it on the page.

REFERENCES: YOUR PAPER'S PEDIGREE

In other sections of this book, I've already presented details about the preparation of reference material in APA format; here, however, I discuss the preparation of your reference list, which immediately follows your Discussion section. The Reference section starts on its own page and, like the rest of the paper, is double-spaced. A reference list is different than a bibliography. In APA format, every reference cited in the research paper must appear in the References section, and every reference in the References section must be cited somewhere in the research paper. The author names and publication years cited in the text must match the References section perfectly. References are presented with a hanging indent, meaning that the first line of the reference is flush left, and every remaining line is indented (you will see this in the sample paper). Note that in Microsoft Word, you can type a reference in APA format, highlight it, and then go to the Paragraph section, and select the hanging indent option (the keyboard shortcut for Windows users is Control-T).

As mentioned earlier, your References section is very important. It shows your academic achievement in completing your research paper; as Smith (2000) stated, the task of preparing citations and references "is, however, one of the most important topics regarding manuscript preparation because through citations and references you make or break your reputation as a careful and thorough scholar" (p. 146). The references you list provide the reader with the trail of your scientific and psychological thought process. Inclusion of seminal works means that you became familiar enough with the literature to know what is important and what is not, which is a characteristic of a developing scholar. In addition, the References section will test your attention to detail because, as previously noted, the rules for presenting reference material in APA format are quite precise. To this end, there are software programs (e.g., EndNote Plus, Mendeley, Zotero) that aid in the bibliographic gathering of reference materials. Some programs also aid in the formatting of research papers or manuscripts. I think these types of programs are fine in helping you track and organize bibliographic citations; however, I would caution you not to use them in manuscript preparation.

Why? First, if you let a computer program do the APA formatting of your references in text and in the References section, then you won't learn the details yourself, similar to how children are taught to do math by hand before they are given a calculator. Second, if your instructor deviates from APA Style, odds are you cannot tell the program to follow some APA format rules and not others. I recommend that you conquer APA formatting of references on your own first, and then later you can use a computer program to ease the workload.

TABLES AT A GLANCE

In the research paper assignment I give to students, I have them create at least one table so that they can practice formatting a table in APA format. There are many good examples of tables in the *Publication Manual*. In an APA-formatted table, text can be single- or double-spaced, and the table should not contain any vertical rules (lines)—only horizontal rules are used for clarity. The *Note* at the end of the table often explains the source of the data in the table or the scales or measures used. The benefit of tables is that complex information can be presented in an efficient manner and in a relatively small amount of space (as compared with presenting the same information in repetitive sentences).

How do you determine when to use a table? It was easy for Rebecca in my research methods class because I required it as part of the assignment. But if you are left to make the decision yourself, how do you decide? Basically, it comes down to our theme of storytelling. Sometimes a table can be quite efficient at telling a complex story. For example, if you want to demonstrate the complexity between variables (say with a significant interaction), showing the patterns of means and standard deviations in a table can be much more efficient than writing it out in your Results section. However, if you want to show the means and standard deviations of a one-way analysis of variance with three levels, a table is not really necessary; that information is easily (and more efficiently) presented in text. How do you decide? You need to determine which approach better tells the story. Your confidence in this decision will develop over time, but if you have questions, ask your instructor or consult your local writing center for advice. Figure 7.1 presents each section of Rebecca's TPART first draft; Figure 7.2 presents my version with grading comments.

SAMPLE RESEARCH PAPER, COMPLETED

I end this chapter with Rebecca's completed final version of her research methods paper (Figure 7.3). As I stated earlier, my goal is to present you with real examples of students' work, not "perfect" work, which is unattainable. You will find errors if you look hard enough, and so would your instructor. Some comments and suggestions that I recommended to Rebecca (which you can see in earlier chapters) were not applied—that's OK, as long as errors were corrected. You and your instructor may find flaws that I missed. This is the imperfect nature of teaching and learning. Although Rebecca started with a good rough draft, the final draft shows marked improvement. This represents the process of learning and skill attainment—perseverance at an unfamiliar task can lead to continual improvement of your scientific writing abilities.

FIGURE 7.1. Title Page, Abstract, References, and Table, Rough Draft (continues)

1

Filter Bubbles: How Social Media Contributes to Social Division

Rebecca Cuthbertson

Department of Psychological Science, Boise State University

PSYC 321 Research Methods

Dr. Eric Landrum

December 8, 2018

FIGURE 7.1. Title Page, Abstract, References, and Table, Rough Draft (continued)

2

Abstract

With social media being so prevalent in society, there could be a relationship between filtered social media use and political division. Survey items were developed to assess whether participants filter out differing opinions on social media and measure their opinion polarization. This study was conducted with participants from introductory psychology sections at a large Western university. A significant relationship was found between individuals who express political opinions on social media and their tendency to filter those who hold opposing views.

Keywords: Social media, filter bubbles, political division, political disagreement

3

References

Hall, J. A. (2016). When is social media use social interaction? Defining mediated social interaction. *New Media & Society, 20*, 162-179. doi:10.1177/1461444816660782

Li, H., Li, L., Gan, C., Liu, Y., Tan, C., & Deng, Z. (2018). Disentangling the factors driving users' continuance intention towards social media: A configurational perspective. *Computers in Human Behavior, 85*, 175-182. doi:10.1016/j.chb.2018.03.048

Pariser, E. (2011). *The filter bubble: How the new personalized web is changing what we read and how we think*. Penguin Books.

Pew Research Center (2016). *Demographics of Social Media Users in 2016*. http://www.pewinternet.org/2016/11/11/social-media-update-2016/

Pew Research Center (2017a). *Fewer now have mix of liberal, conservative views in U.S.* http://www.pewresearch.org/fact-tank/2017/10/23/in-polarized-era-fewer-americans-hold-a-mix-of-conservative-and-liberal-views/

Pew Research Center (2017b). *News use across social media platforms 2017*. Retrieved from http://www.journalism.org/2017/09/07/news-use-across-social-media-platforms-2017/

Sutcliffe, A. G., Binder, J. F., & Dunbar, R. I. (2018). Activity in social media and intimacy in social relationships. *Computers in Human Behavior, 85*, 227-235. doi:10.1016/j.chb.2018.03.050

Yang, J., Barnidge, M., & Rojas, H. (2017). The politics of 'unfriending'; User filtration in response to political disagreement on social media. *Computers in Human Behavior, 70,* 22-29. doi:1016/j.chb.2016.12.079

FIGURE 7.1. Title Page, Abstract, References, and Table, Rough Draft (continued)

4

Table 1

Survey Items with Descriptive Responses

Item	M	SD
1. I often express my social/political opinions on social media.	1.93	1.08
2. I will hide, unfriend, or unfollow people on social media for expressing opinions that are different than mine.	2.05	0.97
3. My opinions on controversial topics can change due to conversations on social media.	2.48	1.08
4. Marijuana should be legalized.	3.43	1.37
5. Politics should not be influenced by religion.	3.59	1.14
6. Politically, I identify as		
7. I use social media daily.		

Note: Items 1-5 were measured using a scale from 1 = *strongly disagree* to 5 = *strongly* agree. For item 6, the response categories are 1= *Republican* (38.7%), 2= *Democrat* (34.7%), 3= *Independent* (26.7%). Item 7 was measured with responses of 1 = *yes* (94.9%) and 2 = *no* (5.1%).

Note. From course research paper by Rebecca Cuthbertson, 2018. Copyright 2018 by Rebecca Cuthbertson. Adapted with permission.

FIGURE 7.2. Title Page, Abstract, References, and Table, With Instructor Edits (continues)

λ | **Field Code Changed** |

| **Formatted:** Font: 11 pt |

Filter Bubbles: How Social Media Contributes to Social Division ---- | **Formatted:** Font: Bold |

Rebecca Cuthbertson

Department of Psychological Science, Boise State University

PSYC 321 Research Methods

Dr. Eric Landrum

December 8, 2018

2

Abstract

With social media being so prevalent in society, there could be a relationship between filtered

social media use and political division. Survey items were developed to assess whether   ---- | **Comment:** Avoid passive voice. |

participants filter out differing opinions on social media and measure their opinion polarization.

This study was conducted with participants from introductory psychology sections at a large

Western university. A significant relationship was found between individuals who express

political opinions on social media and their tendency to filter those who hold opposing views.

Keywords: Social social media, filter bubbles, political division, political disagreement

FIGURE 7.2. Title Page, Abstract, References, and Table, With Instructor Edits (continued)

3

References

Hall, J. A. (2016). When is social media use social interaction? Defining mediated social interaction. *New Media & Society, 20*, 162-179. https://doi.org/~10.1177/1461444816660782

Li, H., Li, L., Gan, C., Liu, Y., Tan, C., & Deng, Z. (2018). Disentangling the factors driving users' continuance intention towards social media: A configurational perspective. *Computers in Human Behavior, 85*, 175-182. doi:https://doi.org/10.1016/j.chb.2018.03.048

Pariser, E. (2011). *The filter bubble: How the new personalized web is changing what we read and how we think*. Penguin Books.

Pew Research Center. (2016). *Demographics of social media users in 2016*. http://www.pewinternet.org/2016/11/11/social-media-update-2016/

Pew Research Center. (2017a). *Fewer now have mix of liberal, conservative views in U.S.* http://www.pewresearch.org/fact-tank/2017/10/23/in-polarized-era-fewer-americans-hold-a-mix-of-conservative-and-liberal-views/

Pew Research Center. (2017b). *News use across social media platforms 2017*. Retrieved from http://www.journalism.org/2017/09/07/news-use-across-social-media-platforms-2017/

Sutcliffe, A. G., Binder, J. F., & Dunbar, R. I. (2018). Activity in social media and intimacy in social relationships. *Computers in Human Behavior, 85*, 227-235. doi:https://doi.org/10.1016/j.chb.2018.03.050

Yang, J., Barnidge, M., & Rojas, H. (2017). The politics of 'unfriending': User filtration in response to political disagreement on social media. *Computers in Human Behavior, 70*, 22-29. doi:https://doi.org/1016/j.chb.2016.12.079

Zilberstein, K. (2015). Technology, relationships, and culture: Clinical and theoretical implications. *Clinical Social Work Journal, 42*, 151-158. doi:https:/doi.org/10.1007/s10615-013-0461-2

Comment: Be sure to include the issue number (in parentheses but not italicized) following the volume number.

Comment: DOI format has changed in the seventh edition of the *Publication Manual*.

FIGURE 7.2. Title Page, Abstract, References, and Table, With Instructor Edits (continued)

Table 1   4

Survey Items ~~w~~<u>W</u>ith Descriptive Responses

Item	M	SD
1. I often express my social/political opinions on social media.	1.93	1.08
2. I will hide, unfriend, or unfollow people on social media for expressing opinions that are different than mine.	2.05	0.97
3. My opinions on controversial topics can change due to conversations on social media.	2.48	1.08
4. Marijuana should be legalized.	3.43	1.37
5. Politics should not be influenced by religion.	3.59	1.14
6. Politically, I identify as		
7. I use social media daily.		

Notes. Items 1-5 were measured using a scale from 1 = *strongly disagree* to 5 = *strongly* agree. For item 6, the response categories are 1 = *Republican* (38.7%), 2 = *Democrat* (34.7%), <u>and</u> 3 = *Independent* (26.7%). Item 7 was measured with responses of 1 = *yes* (94.9%) and 2 = *no* (5.1%).

> **Comment:** *"Note."* would be singular, despite the fact that there are multiple notes.

Note. From course research paper by Rebecca Cuthbertson, 2018. Copyright 2018 by Rebecca Cuthbertson. Adapted with permission.

FIGURE 7.3. Sample Research Paper, Final Draft (continues)

Filter Bubbles: How Social Media Contributes to Social Division

Rebecca Cuthbertson

Department of Psychological Science, Boise State University

PSYC 321 Research Methods

Dr. Eric Landrum

December 8, 2018

FIGURE 7.3. Sample Research Paper, Final Draft (continued)

Abstract

With social media being so prevalent in society, there could be a relationship between filtered social media use and political division. I developed survey items to measure the presence of filtered social media use and participant opinion polarization. This survey study was conducted with participants from introductory psychology sections at a large Western university. A significant relationship exists between individuals who express political opinions on social media and their tendency to filter those who hold opposing views.

Keywords: social media, filter bubbles, political division, political disagreement

FIGURE 7.3. Sample Research Paper, Final Draft (continued)

3

Filter Bubbles: How Social Media Contributes to Social Division

Americans are further apart ideologically now than at any other point in the past 20 years (Pew Research Center, 2017a) and filter bubbles may be to blame (Pariser, 2011). The Pew Research Center (2017a) reported that 32% of U.S. citizens had both liberal and conservative views on social issues compared to 49% in 1994. With social media at the forefront of personal broadcasting, polarizing social opinions can be viewed online. Out of the U.S. adults who use the internet, 79% use Facebook (Pew Research Center, 2016). With social media being so prevalent in society, there could be a relationship between social media and the increase in political division. The filter bubble theory could explain how social media and political division impact one another. Pariser explained that filter bubbles are created by algorithms that personalize what individuals see online, this means that two people could search the same topic and receive differing results. Individuals can contribute to filter bubbles with user filtration options being available on social media platforms—unfollowing, unfriending, blocking. Filter bubbles could lead to each person developing a personalized online experience that keeps new or different information out.

Researchers determined that social media is used more often as social surveillance instead of communication and interaction. Social surveillance means that less time is spent commenting and messaging, and more time is spent scrolling and viewing what people have posted (Hall, 2016). It is not uncommon for social media users to obtain news on social media sites (Pew Research Center, 2017b). After a survey study, researchers found that 74.8% of survey respondents experienced political disagreement on social media (Yang et al., 2016). There is a strong overlap in social networks for online and offline relationships. Researchers proposed that people could be equally selective about whom they interact with offline and online (Sutcliffe et al., 2018). Researchers concluded that enjoyment is what drives social media users to continue using social media sites; social media users are likely to spend more time on social media if they enjoy the content (Li et al., 2018). Trends occur throughout history

FIGURE 7.3. Sample Research Paper, Final Draft (continued)

4

with and without social media; technology performs as a medium for expressing ideas already present in society. Zilberstein (2015) stated that there is little significant evidence that technology weakens social bonds and keeps new ideas from people. However, users constructing an online experience filled with only information that is familiar could lead to intellectual isolation (Pariser, 2011).

Although researchers have reported that social media users encounter political disagreement online, there is little evidence that individuals filter out people they disagree with on social media. If individuals use social media for enjoyment and social surveillance, then social media users could filter out what they do not enjoy or care to see. The purpose of my study is to determine if social media users contribute to filter bubbles that promote intellectual isolation and social division.

An online survey was administered to sections of introductory psychology at a large Western university. I examined whether or not social media users filter out people they disagree with by hiding, unfollowing, and unfriending. Then, I determined if those who filter more often have more polarizing opinions on social issues.

I hypothesize that social media users create filter bubbles. I hypothesize that individuals who use social media filtration will have more polarizing opinions on social issues.

Method

Participants

This study was conducted with 160 participants from introductory psychology sections at a large Western university. Women comprised 66.3% of participants, men 29.4%. Ages ranged from 18 to 30 years, with the mean age of 18.95 years (SD = 1.97). Participants voluntarily completed a survey and were rewarded course credit.

FIGURE 7.3. Sample Research Paper, Final Draft (continued)

5

Materials

I developed survey items to measure the presence of filtered social media use and participant opinion polarization. A pilot test was conducted with students in a research methods class. For the complete list of survey items, refer to Table 1.

Procedure

Participants were self-selected via Sona Systems and completed the survey individually online through Qualtrics. The allotted time to complete the survey was 60 min, with the average completion time being 29.50 min (SD = 16.47). Upon completion, participants were thanked but not debriefed.

Results

I hypothesized that social media users create filter bubbles. The key question of interest will be "I will hide, unfriend, or unfollow people on social media for expressing opinions that are different than mine," which was measured on a scale from 1 = *strongly disagree* to 5 = *strongly agree*. The hypothesis was tested by comparing the key question to the items "I often express my social/political opinions on social media" and "my opinions on controversial topics can change due to conversations on social media"; both were measured on a scale from 1 = *strongly disagree* to 5 = *strongly agree*. There is a statistically significant relationship between answers to the key item and answers to the item "I often express my social/political opinions on social media," $r(157)$ = .26, p = .001. There is a statistically significant relationship between responses to the key item and responses to the item "my opinions on controversial topics can change due to conversations on social media," $r(157)$ = .22, p = .005.

I hypothesized that individuals who hide, unfollow, or unfriend people on social media for expressing different opinions would have more polarizing responses to political questions. The key item is "I will hide, unfriend, or unfollow people on social media for expressing opinions that are different than mine," measured on a scale from 1 = *strongly disagree* to 5 = *strongly agree*. The two political items are "politics should not be influenced by religion" and "marijuana should be legalized," both measured

FIGURE 7.3. Sample Research Paper, Final Draft (continued)

6

on a scale from 1 = *strongly disagree* to 5 = *strongly agree*. To test the hypothesis, key item responses were compared to the responses on the political items. There is not a statistically significant relationship between responses to the key item and responses to the item "politics should not be influenced by religion," $r(157) = -.03$, $p = .678$. There is not a statistically significant relationship between the key item responses and "marijuana should be legalized," $r(157) = -.02$, $p = .795$.

Discussion

The purpose of my study is to assess whether social media users contribute to the construction of filter bubbles on social media. Social media users who express their social and political opinions on social media are more likely to hide, unfriend, or unfollow users who have different political opinions. However, user filtration on social media does not have a significant relationship with polarizing political opinions.

I hypothesized that social media users create filter bubbles. In support of this hypothesis, a significant relationship was found between individuals who express political opinions on social media and their tendency to filter those who hold opposing views. This means that those who express their opinion on social media are more likely to hide, unfriend, and unfollow people who disagree or express opposing opinions. This aligns well with my hypothesis. A significant relationship was found between filtering out opposing views on social media and an individual's capacity to change their opinion due to conversations on social media. This means that individuals who reported filtering out opposing views on social media also reported that their opinions on controversial issues can change due to conversations on social media. This result seems counterintuitive. My assumption is that those who filter out opposing opinions are less likely to change their opinions on controversial topics. This unexpected result could be due to participants being reluctant to admit to having unyielding opinions. Another possibility is that individuals who reported using filtration methods encounter more political conversations on social media than individuals who do not use filtration. If an individual is exposed to more political

FIGURE 7.3. Sample Research Paper, Final Draft (continued)

conversation, they could be more likely to change their views while also being more prone to use filtration methods.

I hypothesized that individuals who hide, unfollow, or unfriend people on social media for expressing different opinions would have more polarizing political opinions. There was not a significant relationship between social media filtration and polarizing opinions. This means that the level of agreement an individual has on social or political issues is not impacted by whether or not they filter out opposing viewpoints.

With the political divide widening (Pew Research Center, 2017a) and social media becoming more prevalent (Pew Research Center, 2016), some individuals have questioned whether there is a relationship between the two. Pariser (2011) explained that filter bubbles are present on social media sites with user filtration options being available. Researchers disclosed that 74.8% of survey respondents experienced political disagreement on social media (Yang et al., 2016). Researchers suggested that there is a strong overlap in social media networks and in-person relationships (Sutcliffe et al., 2018). Research on filter bubbles is limited; there is little evidence that suggests social media users contribute to filter bubbles. In my study, I found a significant relationship between expressing political opinions on social media and filtering differing opinions. This aligns with the thoughts of Pariser (2011); social media users could be contributing to the construction of filter bubbles when confronted with differing beliefs online. Future study items that would help clarify the presence and construction of filter bubbles include: how social media users decide who they are going to interact with online, how often individuals encounter political posts on social media, and how often individuals engage with people offline that have differing social or political views.

Social media users who express their social and political opinions are more likely to hide, unfriend, or unfollow users who have different political opinions. It is important to acknowledge this relationship and address how this could impact social division. Political division has been getting worse

FIGURE 7.3. Sample Research Paper, Final Draft (continued)

8

and filtering out opposing opinions online could be hindering the progression toward common ground. Although I found a relationship between expressing opinions and social media filtration due to disagreement, there was an overwhelming amount of responses from individuals indicating they do not express their ideas online or use filtration methods. When asked "I often express my social/political opinion on social media," 76.3% of participants reported either *disagree* or *strongly disagree*. When asked "I will hide, unfriend, or unfollow people on social media for expressing opinions that are different than mine," 70.9% of participants reported either disagree or *strongly disagree*. These responses were surprising, but I believe that there is a chance that these social media users are already in a filter bubble. I assume that there is a high level of disagreement because these individuals do not feel the need to express their opinions or use filtration methods on social media. I speculate that these individuals do not feel the need to express their opinions or filter information because they are already surrounded by like-minded people on social media. I theorize that the foundation of filter bubbles may be formed offline, then transferred to an online medium and fine-tuned with social media filtration options. In future research, a more in-depth look at the development of social networks and their translation to an online medium could provide further understanding of filter bubbles, online interaction, and social division.

There were limitations on the number of survey items I was able to ask, and there are also corrections I would make to existing survey items. First, I was only able to ask six questions. Under this constraint, the survey items should have been restricted to only questions pertaining to social media filtration—rather than involve polarizing opinions. If the survey items involving polarizing opinions were discarded, this would make room for more questions establishing social media use and filtration. In regard to the current survey items I would change, frequency scales—rather than agreement scales—would have been a better approach for measuring expression of political opinions, the use of social media filters, and whether conversations on social media can change political opinions.

FIGURE 7.3. Sample Research Paper, Final Draft (continued)

9

Social media users who express their social and political opinions on social media are more likely to hide, unfriend, or unfollow users who have different political opinions. This aligns with the theory that social media users aid in the construction of filter bubbles. If further research on filter bubbles were to be conducted, counteracting social division could be possible and progressive conversations could happen.

FIGURE 7.3. Sample Research Paper, Final Draft (continued)

10

References

Hall, J. A. (2016). When is social media use social interaction? Defining mediated social interaction. *New*

    Media & Society, 20(1), 162-179. https://doi.org/10.1177/1461444816660782

Li, H., Li, L., Gan, C., Liu, Y., Tan, C., & Deng, Z. (2018). Disentangling the factors driving users'

    continuance intention towards social media: A configurational perspective. *Computers in Human*

    Behavior, 85, 175-182. https://doi.org/10.1016/j.chb.2018.03.048

Pariser, E. (2011). *The filter bubble: How the new personalized web is changing what we read and how*

    we think. Penguin Books.

Pew Research Center. (2016). *Demographics of social media users in 2016.*

    http://www.pewinternet.org/2016/11/11/social-media-update-2016/

Pew Research Center. (2017a). *Fewer now have mix of liberal, conservative views in U.S.*

    http://www.pewresearch.org/fact-tank/2017/10/23/in-polarized-era-fewer-americans-hold-a-

    mix-of-conservative-and-liberal-views/

Pew Research Center. (2017b). *News use across social media platforms 2017.*

    http://www.journalism.org/2017/09/07/news-use-across-social-media-platforms-2017/

Sutcliffe, A. G., Binder, J. F., & Dunbar, R. I. (2018). Activity in social media and intimacy in social

    relationships. *Computers in Human Behavior, 85*, 227-235.

    https://doi.org/10.1016/j.chb.2018.03.050

Yang, J., Barnidge, M., & Rojas, H. (2017). The politics of 'unfriending': User filtration in response to

    political disagreement on social media. *Computers in Human Behavior, 70,* 22-29.

    https://doi.org/10.1016/j.chb.2016.12.079

Zilberstein, K. (2015). Technology, relationships, and culture: Clinical and theoretical implications.

    Clinical Social Work Journal, 42, 151-158. https://doi.org/10.1007/s10615-013-0461-2

FIGURE 7.3. Sample Research Paper, Final Draft (continued)

11

Table 1

Survey Items With Descriptive Responses

Item	M	SD
1. I often express my social/political opinions on social media.	1.93	1.08
2. I will hide, unfriend, or unfollow people on social media for expressing opinions that are different than mine.	2.05	0.97
3. My opinions on controversial topics can change due to conversations on social media.	2.48	1.08
4. Marijuana should be legalized.	3.43	1.37
5. Politics should not be influenced by religion.	3.59	1.14
6. Politically, I identify as		
7. I use social media daily.		

Note. Items 1-5 were measured using a scale from 1 = *strongly disagree* to 5 = *strongly* agree. For item 6, the response categories are 1 = *Republican* (38.7%), 2 = *Democrat* (34.7%), and 3 = *Independent* (26.7%). Item 7 was measured with responses of 1 = *yes* (94.9%) and 2 = *no* (5.1%).

Reshaping Your Story for Different Audiences

Other Types of Writing in Psychology

But the familiarity of bad academic writing raises a puzzle. Why should a profession that trades in words and dedicates itself to the transmission of knowledge so often turn out prose that is turgid, soggy, wooden, bloated, clumsy, obscure, unpleasant to read, and impossible to understand?

—STEVEN PINKER, *WHY ACADEMICS STINK AT WRITING*

The bulk of this book has been devoted to scientific writing and its many forms in psychology courses. This final chapter briefly presents other types of writing that you may encounter as an undergraduate student. This is certainly not meant to be an exhaustive list of all the other types of writing; here, the specific focus is on (a) writing for presentations at conferences, (b) writing your resume or curriculum vitae, (c) writing for the internet (i.e., blogging, posting to social media such as Facebook, Twitter, and Instagram), and (d) writing for pleasure and insight.

PRESENTING AT CONFERENCES

As an undergraduate student, you may have the opportunity to present the outcomes of a class project or research paper at a conference. Such conferences are held locally (sometimes), statewide, regionally, nationally, and even internationally. As part of good science, psychologists gather on a frequent basis to share information and present the findings of our latest research. To acculturate students to this environment, many psychology conferences have student sections during which students participate in the same types of tasks as professional psychologists, such as giving an oral paper presentation or participating in a poster session.

An oral presentation at a conference usually includes a student speaking to an audience for about 12 to 15 minutes (a conference poster presentation is different and is covered in the next section). Here, you are making an oral presentation to the audience about your research paper or project. Your goal is to give an engaging presentation of the outcomes of your research. The next two paragraphs include suggestions from Karlin (2000) and Landrum and Davis (2020) on how to deliver your presentation.

A safe opening is to read the title of your presentation, introduce yourself, and be sure to thank any others who contributed to the project. Do not read your presentation, but have notes prepared for every section of it. A very logical sequence would be Introduction, Method, Results, and Discussion—sound familiar? Remember to speak slowly and clearly, but not in a monotone. You know from listening to your professors who sounds good and who doesn't—try to copy the presentation style you find most informative. Consider the big picture. What are the main ideas and findings of your study? Decide on a limited number of significant ideas that you want your audience to comprehend and remember.

In Chapter 7, I presented a sample paper from my student Rebecca. Let's say that she has now decided to present her paper at a conference during an oral presentation session. It would be pretty boring for the audience to sit and listen to her read her paper word for word; a better strategy would be for her to extract the most useful information and tell the audience a compelling story about her research and what she found. Instead of reading the Introduction to the audience, she might say the following:

> Do you think that when you are cruising around on Facebook or Twitter, the stories and images that are appearing in your feed pop up in a random order? Do you believe that how these stories are presented to you has no impact on your behavior or the behavior of others, say, in the area of product purchasing or voting for a U.S. President? We each live in a social media filter bubble, and it is important to understand how that bubble influences our own behavior, whether we realize the influence or not. This is what I decided to study.

By setting up the story in this fashion, audience members should be curious to know how the results turn out. A compelling story captures our attention (Kendall-Tackett, 2007) and makes us desire closure; we want to know how the story (or in this case, the results of the study) turned out.

You should dress nicely in business professional attire. If it makes sense for your presentation, try to engage the audience in a brief activity related to your study—it's a great way to encourage your audience to be active participants in your presentation. Prepare PowerPoint slides to keep your audience engaged. These visual aids should be simple and large enough for individuals in the back of the room to see. As a general rule, don't use anything smaller than 18-point font; 24-point font is even better. Try to speak loudly and clearly enough to hold your audience's attention. There will be distractions—people coming in, others getting up and leaving. Don't be offended. Try to be enthusiastic enough to sustain interest over these distractions. State your final conclusions and end on time. Be prepared to answer audience questions if time permits. No one will purposely try to stump you with a question. However, if you do not know the answer, say "I don't know." If you want to speculate, that's okay, but tell the audience that it is only your speculation.

Students who present during a conference experience what it is like to be a scientist sharing their results with an audience. Although a bit nerve-racking at first, your 12–15 minutes will go by quickly, and the professional experience is invaluable. However, if you are not quite ready to give an oral presentation but you have research to present at a conference, there is another option, and it is one used by faculty researchers and students alike—the conference poster presentation.

A poster presentation is substantially different from a paper presentation. In a paper presentation, you present your findings to an audience in a relatively short time period. The method is somewhat impersonal, but it is an efficient method to present the materials to a large number of people. In a poster presentation, you present your research work in a poster format for a longer period of time (1–2 hours). You are available to speak personally with "audience members" who are interested in your work. You will probably reach fewer people with a poster session, but you'll have more personal conversations with people who are genuinely interested in your work. Posters are typically displayed on a free-standing bulletin board in a session with other posters, in a room large enough to hold the posters, the presenters, and the people who wander through the session. The audience members (conference attendees) pick and choose which posters to read; they can acquire more detailed information from the poster authors in this one-on-one conversation format.

There are a number of resources available to help you design your poster, including valuable tips in this chapter. The Psi Chi website (https://www.psichi. org/page/RES_ConvPosCheck#.XkF5P1VKiUk) provides nice resources to help students prepare posters and know what to expect regarding a poster presentation during a conference session. You can also find helpful templates for designing posters in PowerPoint (see https://templates.office.com/en-us/Science-project-poster-TM00001151; you'll see they call it a science project poster).

As a general rule, I prefer to prepare a poster from a completed manuscript, such as a research paper. Essentially, the text of the paper becomes the text of the poster, but in a shortened format. The text provided in a poster can only be enough to provide a context for the study. The goal of your poster session is to engage audience members as they stop by to talk. You can provide them with a complete copy of your poster or paper, but the key is conversation. You can learn much about your research and that of others by talking to professionals about your research. I have often gotten an idea for the next study just by presenting my research at a poster session. Here are some tips for preparing a conference poster (some from Szuchman, 2005) and some outlines of how a poster might be designed (Figures 8.1, 8.2, and 8.3; Western Psychological Association, 2020). Figure 8.4 displays a sample of a poster I presented with a student coauthor, Cierra Abellera.

FIGURE 8.1. Sample Poster Layout

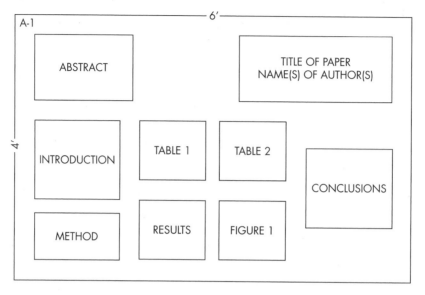

Note. Copyright 2020 by the Western Psychological Association. Reprinted with permission.

FIGURE 8.2. Sample Poster Layout

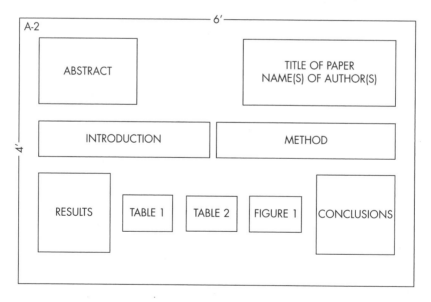

Note. Copyright 2020 by the Western Psychological Association. Reprinted with permission.

Construct the poster to include the title, author(s), affiliation(s), and a description of the research. Your poster should be readable from a distance of 3 feet. Posters are true to the spirit of American Psychological Association format, but the rules of presentation are relaxed. Minimize the detail that is presented and try to use jargon-free statements. Pictures, tables, and figures are

FIGURE 8.3. Sample Poster Layout

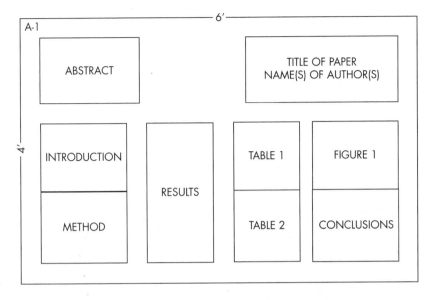

Note. Copyright 2020 by the Western Psychological Association. Reprinted with permission.

especially useful and helpful in poster presentations. During your poster presentation, wear your name badge and make sure it is visible to conference attendees. Be ready to put up and take down your poster at the specified times (you may want to bring your own thumbtacks or pushpins); poster sessions are often scheduled back to back, so you want to end on time so the next session can begin on time. Bring 30 to 50 copies of your handouts to provide more information about your study and your contact information. And finally, you may be on your feet for 1 to 2 hours, so wear comfortable shoes! Note that the example poster in Figure 8.4 is text heavy and probably not the best-designed poster (yes, sometimes I don't practice what I preach). However, it does illustrate the various sections you should have in any poster presentation.

WRITING YOUR RESUME OR CURRICULUM VITAE

When students think about writing and writing assignments, they probably do not think about the necessity of writing a resume or a curriculum vitae (CV). However, by the time you leave your college or university, you will likely need one or both of these two documents. Let's start here—what *is* the difference between a resume and a CV? A resume is typically laser-focused, 1–2 pages long, and highlights the preparer's educational background and employment history (Cassuto, 2019; Kawar et al., 2017). Industry leaders who study human resources trends advise that one's resume should focus on impact on an organization, with a special emphasis on providing data and examples to support claims of impact (Economy, 2020). And what shouldn't your resume have?

FIGURE 8.4. Example of a Poster Session

Development of the Campus and Career Resources Inventory

Eastern Psychological Association, New York City, NY
March 1, 2019

Cierra Abellera and R. Eric Landrum

Department of Psychological Science

BOISE STATE UNIVERSITY

Abstract

The purpose of our research is to understand students' use of undergraduate psychology resources. In a national study of four universities, 7 psychology-specific resources were evaluated in conjunction with student career paths. Students primarily rely on faculty to obtain accurate information on their intended careers whereas student clubs and organizations were rated as one of the lowest in importance to advancing student career paths. Additionally, all seven resources were reported as average in helping students efficiently.

Career exploration is a critical task during the development of young adults which is essential in leading satisfying postgraduate lives (Lee, Porfeli, & Hirschi, 2016; Showkeir & Workwise, 2017). According to a national survey of psychology graduates, the National Center for Science and Engineering Statistics found the following top ten common occupations for psychology majors with a bachelor's in psychology: 1) administrative occupations, 2) management-related occupations, 3) service occupations excluding health (probation officer, human services), 4) social workers, 5) top-level managers, execs, admins (CEO/COO/CFO, president, director, manager, provost), 6) teachers and instructors (private tutors, dance, martial arts), 7) marketing and sales occupations, 8) personnel, training, and labor relations specialist, 9) accountants, auditors, and other financial specialists, and 10) accounting clerks and bookkeepers (National Science Foundation, 2015). The job descriptions provided above gave a broad sense of careers primarily entered by psychology graduates with a bachelor's degree as their highest degree however, there is no further insight into specific job titles and relevance to their degree.

Method

There was a total of 235 participants, 144 participants attended Boise State University, 66 participants attended James Madison University, 17 participants attended Texas A&M University–Kingsville, and 8 participants attended the University of Wisconsin–Green Bay. Of the participants, 55% identified as female and 45% identified as male. There were 156 participants between the age range of 18–29 and 9 participants between the ages of 30–53. Twenty-two percent of participants self-identified as first-generation students. Participants were also asked their first pathway after receiving a bachelor's degree in psychology in which 15.9% intended to enter the psychology workforce, 45.5% intended to pursue graduate school in psychology, 18.3% intended to pursue a professional school in an area outside of psychology, and 17.9% were undecided at the time of the survey. In a set of matched type questions (e.g. open- and close-ended), we assessed each of the following: whether each resource was known to the student, importance and relevance to the student's career path, an estimated amount of time spent using the resource, the student's perception of their ability to effectively use each resource, and how this resource could be more efficient in providing accurate knowledge and/or support towards the student's intended career.

Results

Campus resources were evaluated for helpfulness, importance, and self-efficacy. The faculty were consistently rated as most helpful in career advancement when compared to the department, Career Center, and student psychology clubs/

organizations. Importance and self-efficacy were average in overall career advancement and in making the most of the interactions.

Table 1

	Department	Faculty	Career Center	Student Psychology Clubs/Organizations
Helping you advance (%-es)	57.0	75.3	38.3	26.8
Importance to overall career advancement*	2.62 (0.8)	2.94 (0.8)	2.62 (0.9)	2.42 (0.8)
Self Efficiency**	3.23 (1.0)	3.49 (1.0)	3.26 (1.0)	3.10 (1.0)

*The item was rated on a 4-point scale from 1 = not at all important to 4 = extremely important. **This item was asked on a 5-point Likert-type scale from 1 = strongly disagree to 5 = strongly agree.

The diagram to the right displays the O*NET OnLine survey results per item. When compared to O*NET OnLine, APA Graduate Study in Psychology, and CareerOneStop, O*NET OnLine was the most well-known resource with 41.2% of students knowing the resource existed. O*NET OnLine had the highest percentage of usage when compared to the above resources. All three resources were reported to perform as average in helpfulness in advancing students' career paths. Students reported their self-efficacy as average in all three resources.

in Psychology and CareerOneShop. Most survey respondents were Boise State University students where O*NET OnLine is introduced to all psychology undergraduates through an introduction to the major course and could be a potential explanation for O*NET high knowledge rating. On average, students reported that these resources were about average in helping them advance their career paths and consistently reported lower self-efficiency in using the resources. Since there is not a resource that is reported to excel in supporting undergraduates in pursuing their career paths, there is a need for improved access to accurate and informative resources.

Discussion

Although the Campus and Career Resource Inventory broadly illustrates the evaluation of resources for psychology undergraduates, there is room for improvement to include more specific resources such as professional mentorship, other organization memberships such as the Association for Psychological Science student affiliate status, and networking experiences. Additionally, to assess helpfulness in future studies using this inventory, campus-related resources should be measured on a scale instead of asking participants to respond either "yes" or "no" to the item. The psychology-specific resources that were not campus-specific were APA Graduate Study in Psychology, O*NET OnLine, and CareerOneStop. For these resources, 41.7% of students reported knowing that O*NET OnLine existed as a resource followed by the APA Graduate Study

Current experts suggest that resumes do not need to include the "Objectives" section; it provides little added value, and when near the top of the resume, it can be a wasted opportunity for a strong first impression (Burnison, 2019).

In today's economy, companies large and small can be inundated with applications when advertising for job openings. This means a flood of cover letters and resumes for companies to review, and many of those companies now rely on applicant tracking systems, or ATS. A human resources manager would enter keywords based on desired skills and characteristics regarding the job search—then the ATS would scan the database of received resumes for matches and return the highest percentage matches. In an overview article about this process, Sleigh and Ritzer (2020) provided some tips for resume preparers about how to navigate your path successfully if you are submitting your resume to a company using an ATS:

1. Identify the keywords used in the job advertisement, and repeat those keywords as appropriate throughout your resume.

2. Simplify the resume formatting; do not change fonts, do not use abbreviations (like APA), and make sure you follow file format instructions exactly.

3. As always, make sure there are no spelling or typographical errors.

4. Include a cover letter, unless the instructions specifically prohibit the inclusion of a cover letter. After ATS screening, the next level is (hopefully) for a human to review your materials, including the cover letter.

5. Keep networking, which also includes getting feedback about your application materials (cover letter, resume).

For more tips about coordinating the cover letter and resume, with a special emphasis on promoting your skills, see Spencer (2020).

The CV is a bit different from the resume, as it is intended to be more comprehensive and does not follow the typical 1–2 page limitation. The CV should include awards, achievements, and recognitions (Kawar et al., 2017), or as Cassuto (2019) would put it, the CV should be a combination of salesmanship and autobiography. In thinking about the sections of your CV, consider the following:

- Personal/contact information

- Education/credentials (expected/anticipated graduation date clearly indicated)

- Honors and awards (including scholarships, Dean's list)

- Educational experiences (including research assistantships, teaching assistantships, internships, service learning opportunities, study abroad experiences)

- Professional experiences (conference presentations [oral, poster, symposia], manuscripts submitted for publication, published journal articles)

- Professional memberships (organizations and clubs, on- or off-campus, including leadership positions held)

- Work experiences (work history overlapping with college, applicable military experience; complete work history can be provided upon request)

WRITING FOR THE INTERNET (INCLUDING BLOGGING, FACEBOOK, TWITTER, AND INSTAGRAM)

In addition to the more typical outlets for scientific works, such as journal articles, books, oral conference presentations, and poster sessions, the internet has indeed become a powerful force in communicating scientific information at a rapid rate. Of course, all of the concerns about the accuracy and veracity of information on the internet still apply, and ensuring the author's credibility is of utmost importance. But the internet allows for almost worldwide availability of information, including valuable scientific information. If your goal is to communicate the results of your research using this vehicle, there are some things to know about writing for the internet and about distribution channels regarding reaching your audiences of interest.

Tips for Thinking About Starting a Blog

The blog form allows writers to share the discipline of psychology and new research findings with a wide audience that might not have access to library journal subscriptions. It can also promote a healthy and balanced dialog of discussion about an issue, and it gives researchers a new forum to present their own research findings to an interested audience (Zou & Hyland, 2020). There is even empirical research emerging about the effectiveness of different practices used in the preparation and distribution of blog posts. Gardiner et al. (2018) reported that when text-only blogs were compared with those that included humor, images, or videos, image-based blogs resulted in superior recall and enjoyment for their readers.

Zou and Hyland (2020) described the following key methods for blog writers to engage with blog readers:

- reader mention: addressing readers casually in the text, as you know you would, as demonstrated here in this bullet point using second-person pronouns

- directives: giving instructions or imploring the reader to step into action

- questions: engaging the reader directly with a conversational tone and give-and-take

- shared knowledge markers: hooking or bringing the reader into the story with a familiar example or situation

- personal asides: including a personal comment, meant to relate the writer to the reader, to show a personal glimpse of the "real" person who is writing.

Beyond the strategies suggested here regarding how to write within the blog structure, Jarreau (2017) also strategized about how to attract a general following to your science communication efforts in general. Jarreau's recommendations were to (a) follow on social media those individuals or organizations you are trying to reach; (b) be the creator of new, valued, and engaging content for those individuals or organizations you are trying to reach; and (c) actually interact with those individuals and organizations you are trying to reach. Do the work to do the networking. None of this is easy, but neither is getting your work noticed and published. Fortunately, there are an increasing number of methods for being noticed in the modern world, and this next section provides some insights on how to achieve those goals on social media in an effective yet socially responsible manner.

Tips for Writing Social Media Posts

Scientists are becoming more and more engaged in social media (Savage, 2015; "Social Media for Scientists," 2018), and there are even formal definitions emerging as to what constitutes a "scientific tweet." Collins et al. (2016) suggested three criteria for a scientific tweet: content is scientific in nature, tweet is issued by a scientist, and tweet is accompanied by a science-type hashtag (e.g., #science).

There are a number of potential social media outlets for scientists, and some will be more familiar than others. Table 8.1 presents some of these outlets and a brief description.

If you were going to start writing for a blog, or posting to a social media site, what would that be like? The easiest way to figure that out is to create an account and start following people or topics that interest you (ideally both). You can give science communication as much or as little of your intellectual life as you want.

On social media, the best stories tend to be short stories (Lewis, 2018). When thinking about stories, remember that the keys are setting up and resolving the conflict. In a movie, this conflict is between two characters (typically); in psychology, the conflict is often between two competing theories or conflicting predictions about what will happen with the dependent variable. Resolving the scientific problem means coming to a conclusion about that original hypothesis from which we started our study.

Another technique recommended by Lewis (2018) for telling a good story in science education is called "and–but–therefore." With this style of storytelling, the "and" is the setup of the details of the story, the "but" is the conflict and the problem to be resolved, and the "therefore" is the discussion and resolution of the conflict with the outcome of the research study (in this instance). The classic methods of storytelling are good for the classroom (Landrum, Brakke, &

TABLE 8.1. Social Media Outlets With Brief Functional Descriptions

Social media type/site	Description/function
Twitter	A social networking site with 140- to 280-character messages or "tweets." A person follows the tweets of others (friends, colleagues, scientists, acquaintances, strangers) and can be followed back. Messages can be "retweeted" and shared and commented on. Private lists can be curated and direct (private) messages can be sent.
Facebook	A social networking site where you can post a profile, text, photos, videos, and links to other individuals, labs, and websites. A Facebook page can be dedicated to a lab, a singular person, a topic, or a research group, and can be followed by anyone. Group discussions (moderated or unmoderated) and direct (private) messaging are available.
Blogging	Writing relatively short articles for public consumption, for example, sharing private journal thoughts about a topic the writer is passionate about, on a website specifically designed to display blog content. The blog forum typically has the capability for commenting and archiving of past blog entries.
Instagram	Social networking site that is oriented toward displaying images rather than being focused on the textual presentation of information. Videos are also common. There is often cross-over posting of materials on both Twitter and Instagram (some software/apps specifically do this: e.g., Hootsuite).
YouTube	A website where original content creators can share and distribute video content through a robust network; users can subscribe to channels and be alerted of new content. Videos can be monetized with advertising on YouTube within regulations.
Reddit	A social networking site where users submit news and content links on a variety of information topics, and also comment on those topics via online discussions.
LinkedIn	A professional networking site that is focused on providing workplace training and professional support via the connections that exist between individuals and the new connections that are made via job applications, collaborations, partnerships, and the like. It is also a website where employers post jobs and job seekers post resumes.

Note. From *Scientist's Guide to Social Media*, by the Association for the Sciences of Limnology and Oceanography, 2019 (https://www.aslo.org/science-communication/scientist-guide-to-social-media/). Copyright 2019 by the Association for the Sciences of Limonology and Oceanography. Adapted with permission.

McCarthy, 2019) and good for science communication on the internet—some methods are just tried and true.

WRITING FOR PLEASURE AND INSIGHT

Even though our focus has been on scientific writing, in this chapter we have explored related types of writing, including writing for conferences (oral and poster presentations), the internet, and essay exams. Back in Chapter 1, I presented the six major categories of writing: expository, descriptive, persuasive, poetic, technical, and narrative (Copywriting in Action School, 2019). Writing is a powerful tool that humans exclusively possess, and we all have stories to tell or information to share. This tool analogy is not uncommon, as Zinsser (1988) wrote in his well-known book *Writing to Learn:*

> Writing is a tool that enables people in every discipline to wrestle facts and ideas. It's a physical activity, unlike reading. Writing requires us to operate some kind of mechanism—pencil, pen, typewriter, word processor—for getting our thoughts on paper. It compels us by the repeated effort of language to go after those thoughts and to organize them and present them clearly. It forces us to keep asking, "Am I saying what I want to say?" (p. 49)

As you think more broadly about writing, I encourage you to explore the beauty and simplicity of writing as a creative and insightful means of self-expression. Although you may not find joy in scientific writing at first, with practice it can actually happen. Pursue other avenues of writing that are more pleasurable for you—perhaps writing short stories, working on a family genealogy, or writing your own science fiction. Writing is an important creative outlet for human beings; even scientific writing, in the way that information is combined and hypotheses are formed and tested, can be creative.

In addition to writing for pleasure, insight, and inspiration, physical and mental health professionals use writing exercises as a healing technique (Gaschler, 2007), especially with veterans (Frankfurt et al., 2019). In a classic study by Pennebaker et al. (1988), 50 healthy undergraduate students wrote about either traumatic events or superficial topics for 20 minutes a day, 3 to 4 days in a row, for 6 weeks. Students writing about traumatic events reported improved moods and fewer illnesses than those in the control group. Other researchers have shown that this type of expressive writing can reduce doctor visits, improve grades, and lead to other positive outcomes (Slatcher & Pennebaker, 2006).

Additionally, when patients experiencing fibromyalgia (a disorder involving muscle pain, stiffness, and fatigue) were instructed to write about personal traumatic events, they experienced short-term psychological and physical health benefits as compared with a control group (Broderick et al., 2005). Stanton et al. (2002) also found that patients with early stage breast cancer had fewer medical visits as a result of writing about their emotions (compared with controls). In another example of the beneficial effects of writing about stressful life experiences, Smyth et al. (1999) found that this type of writing reduced the symptoms of those with asthma or rheumatoid arthritis (a type of arthritis that leads to the destruction of the joints). Each of these studies had control groups that wrote about other topics, so it is not just the act of writing that helps relieve pain, but rather writing about stressful experiences and traumatic events.

The ability to communicate via writing is a quality and trait to be honored, accepted, and practiced. Make the time to write for yourself, as well as practicing your scientific writing in psychology. Remember that writing can lift our spirits and allow us to explore ideas and places worth visiting.

In an article about writing productivity for scientists, Peterson et al. (2018) collected these ideas about writing from other writers. Giving credit where credit is due, I leave you with these insightful words about writing:

- You can't think yourself out of a writing block; you have to write yourself out of a thinking block. (John Rogers)

- Amateurs sit and wait for inspiration, the rest of us just get up and go to work. (Stephen King)

- Almost all good writing begins with terrible first efforts. You need to start somewhere. (Anne Lamott)

- This is how you do it: You sit down at the keyboard and you put one word after another until it's done. It's that easy, and that hard. (Neil Gaiman)

REFERENCES

American Psychological Association. (n.d.-a). *APA PsycExtra quick facts*. https://apa.org/pubs/databases/psycextra/?tab=3

American Psychological Association. (n.d.-b). *APA PsycInfo quick facts*. https://apa.org/pubs/databases/psycinfo/?tab=3

American Psychological Association. (2013). *APA guidelines for the undergraduate psychology major: Version 2.0*. https://www.apa.org/ed/precollege/about/psymajor-guidelines.pdf

American Psychological Association. (2020). *Publication manual of the American Psychological Association* (7th ed.).

Appelcline, K. (n.d.). *The elements of good storytelling*. https://www.skotos.net/articles/GoodStorytelling.html

Association for the Sciences of Limnology and Oceanography. (n.d.). *Scientist guide to social media*. https://www.aslo.org/science-communication/scientist-guide-to-social-media/

Baker, D. S., & Henrichsen, L. (2002). *APA reference style: Introduction*. Brigham Young University. https://linguistics.byu.edu/faculty/henrichsenl/apa/APA02.html

Ballon, R. (2005). *Blueprint for screenwriting: A complete writer's guide to story structure and character development*. Erlbaum.

Bellquist, J. E. (1993). *A guide to grammar and usage for psychology and related fields*. Erlbaum.

Bem, D. J. (2004). Writing the empirical journal article. In J. M. Darley, M. P. Zanna, & H. L. Roediger III (Eds.), *The compleat academic: A career guide* (2nd ed., pp. 185–219). American Psychological Association.

Bentley, M., Peerenboom, C. A., Hodge, F. W., Passano, E. B., Warren, H. C., & Washburn, M. F. (1929). Instructions in regard to preparation of manuscript. *Psychological Bulletin, 26*(2), 57–63. https://doi.org/10.1037/h0071487

Blumenthal, A. L. (1991). The intrepid Joseph Jastrow. In G. A. Kimble, M. Wetheimer, & C. White (Eds.), *Portraits of pioneers in psychology* (pp. 75–87). American Psychological Association.

Bordens, K. S., & Abbott, B. B. (2004). *Research design and methods: A process approach* (5th ed.). McGraw-Hill.

Brewer, B. W., Scherzer, C. B., Van Raalte, J. L., Petitpas, A. J., & Andersen, M. B. (2001). The elements of (APA) style: A survey of psychology journal editors: Comment. *American Psychologist, 56*(3), 266–267. https://doi.org/10.1037/0003-066X.56.3.266

Broderick, J. E., Junghaenel, D. U., & Schwartz, J. E. (2005). Written emotional expression produces health benefits in fibromyalgia patients. *Psychosomatic Medicine, 67*(2), 326–334. https://doi.org/10.1097/01.psy.0000156933.04566.bd

Brunsvold, L. (2003). *LEO thesis statement*. St. Cloud State University. https://leo.stcloudstate.edu/acadwrite/thesistatement.html

Burke, K. S., & Prieto, L. R. (2019). High-quality research training environments and undergraduate psychology students. *Scholarship of Teaching and Learning in Psychology, 5*(3), 223–235. https://doi.org/10.1037/stl0000156

Burnison, G. (2019, December 12). *After 20 years of hiring, I refuse to look at resumes that have this common yet outdated section*. CNBC make it. https://www.cnbc.com/2019/12/09/dont-make-this-common-resume-mistake-here-are-examples-of-what-to-do-instead-says-hiring-ceo.html

Calderón, R. F., & Austin, J. T. (2006). Writing in APA Style: Why and how. In F. T. L. Leong & J. T. Austin (Eds.), *The psychology research handbook: A guide for graduate students and research assistants* (2nd ed., pp. 345–359). https://doi.org/10.4135/9781412976626.n23

Cassuto, L. C. (2019, July 21). *8 tips to improve your CV*. The Chronicle of Higher Education. https://www.chronicle.com/article/8-Tips-to-Improve-Your-CV/246720

Clarivate Analytics. (2020). *Web of science*. http://www.wokinfo.com

Collins, K., Shiffman, D., & Rock, J. (2016). How are scientists using social media in the workplace? *PLOS ONE, 11*(10), e0162680. https://doi.org/10.1371/journal.pone.0162680

Copywriting in Action School. (2019). *The 6 genres of copy writing for selling and telling [Part 1]*. https://copywritinginaction.com.au/copywriting-genres/

Council of Writing Program Administrators. (2003*). Defining and avoiding plagiarism: The WPA statement on best practices* [Handout]. Purdue University.

Crawford, H. J., & Christensen, L. B. (1995). *Developing research skills: A laboratory manual* (3rd ed.). Allyn & Bacon.

Economy, P. (2020, January 13). *Google's career experts say that your resume should always have 5 things*. Business Insider. https://www.businessinsider.com/googles-career-experts-say-that-your-resume-should-have-5-things

Eisenberg, N. (2000). Writing a literature review. In R. J. Sternberg (Ed.), *Guide to publishing in psychology journals* (pp. 17–34). Cambridge University Press. https://doi.org/10.1017/CBO9780511807862.003

Empire State College. (n.d.). *Revising and proofreading the draft*. https://www.esc.edu/online-writing-center/resources/research/research-paper-steps/revising-proofreading/

Fallon, M., Mahon, M. A., & Coyle, M. (2018). Watching screencasts help students learn APA format better than reading the manual. *Teaching of Psychology, 45*(4), 324–332. https://doi.org/10.1177/0098628318796415

Festinger, L. (1957). *A theory of cognitive dissonance*. Row, Peterson.

Frankfurt, S., Frazier, P., Litz, B. T., Schnurr, P. P., Orazem, R. J., Gravely, A., & Sayer, N. (2019). Online expressive writing intervention for reintegration difficulties among veterans: Who is most likely to benefit? *Psychological Trauma: Theory, Research, Practice, and Policy, 11*(8), 861–868. https://doi.org/10.1037/tra0000462

Gallagher, L. A. (Ed.). (2007). *Thesaurus of psychological index terms* (11th ed.). American Psychological Association.

Galvan, J. L. (2006). Guidelines for writing a first draft. In *Writing literature reviews: A guide for students of the social and behavioral sciences* (3rd ed., pp. 81–90). Pyrczak.

Gardiner, A., Sullivan, M., & Grand, A. (2018). Who are you writing for? Differences in response to blog design between scientists and nonscientists. *Science Communication, 40*(1), 109–123. https://doi.org/10.1177/1075547017747608

Gaschler, K. (2007, August). The power of the pen. *Scientific American Mind, 18(4),* 14–15. https://doi.org/10.1038/scientificamericanmind0807-14

Gottschalk, K., & Hjortshoj, K. (2004). *The elements of teaching writing: A resource for instructors in all disciplines.* Bedford/St. Martin's.

Greenberg, K. P. (2015). Rubric use in formative assessment: A detailed behavioral rubric helps students improve their scientific writing skills. *Teaching of Psychology, 42*(3), 211–217. https://doi.org/10.1177/0098628315587618

Harris, R. A. (2005). *Using sources effectively: Strengthening your writing and avoiding plagiarism* (2nd ed.). Pyrczak.

Hibbard, C. S. (n.d.). *How to proofread your own writing.* Cypress Media Group. https://cypressmedia.net/articles/article/14/how_to_proofread_your_own_writing

Hiroshi, S. (1997). *What is Occam's razor?* University of California, Riverside. http://math.ucr.edu/home/baez/physics/General/occam.html

How experts communicate. (2000). Editorial. *Nature Neuroscience, 3,* 97. https://doi.org/10.1038/72151

Jarreau, P. B. (2017, January 15). *3 secrets to social media for science communication.* From the lab bench [Blog]. https://www.fromthelabbench.com/from-the-lab-bench-science-blog/2017/1/15/3-secrets-to-social-media-for-science-communication

Karlin, N. J. (2000). Creating an effective conference presentation. *Eye on Psi Chi, 4*(2), 26–27. https://doi.org/10.24839/1092-0803.Eye4.2.26

Kawar, L. N., Dunbar, G., & Scruth, E. A. (2017). Creating a credible and ethical curriculum vitae. *Clinical Nurse Specialist, 31*(6), 298–303. https://doi.org/10.1097/NUR.0000000000000327

Kendall, P. C., Silk, J. S., & Chu, B. C. (2000). Introducing your research report: Writing the introduction. In R. J. Sternberg (Ed.), *Guide to publishing in psychology journals* (pp. 41–57). Cambridge University Press. https://doi.org/10.1017/CBO9780511807862.005

Kendall-Tackett, K. A. (2007). *How to write for a general audience: A guide for academics who want to share their knowledge with the world and have fun doing it.* American Psychological Association.

Kidd, S., Meyer, C. L., & Olesko, B. M. (2000). *An instructor's guide to electronic databases of indexed professional literature.* Society for the Teaching of Psychology.

Landau, J. D. (n.d.). *Teaching tips: Understanding and preventing plagiarism.* Association for Psychological Science. https://www.psychologicalscience.org/teaching/tips/tips_0403.cfm

Landrum, R. E. (2003). Graduate admissions in psychology: Transcripts and the effect of withdrawals. *Teaching of Psychology, 30*(2), 323–325.

Landrum, R. E., Brakke, K., & McCarthy, M. A. (2019). The pedagogical power of storytelling. *Scholarship of Teaching and Learning in Psychology, 5*(3), 247–253. https://doi.org/10.1037/stl0000152

Landrum, R. E., & Davis, S. F. (2020). *The psychology major: Career options and strategies for success* (6th ed.). Pearson.

Landrum, R. E., Gurung, R. A. R., & Amsel, E. (2019). The importance of taking psychology: A comparison of three levels of exposure. *Teaching of Psychology, 46*(4), 290–298. https://doi.org/10.1177/0098628319872574

Landrum, R. E., & Muench, D. M. (1994). Assessing students' library skills and knowledge: The Library Research Strategies Questionnaire. *Psychological Reports, 75*(3_suppl), 1619–1628. https://doi.org/10.2466/pr0.1994.75.3f.1619

Langston, W. (2002). *Research methods laboratory manual for psychology.* Wadsworth.

Lewis, A. (2018, February 9). *What actually is 'storytelling' in educational social media?* Medium. https://medium.com/communicating-science-with-social-media/what-actually-is-storytelling-in-educational-social-media-7692f74ec5e6

Lipkewich, A. E. (2001). *ABC's of the writing process—Editing*. Westmount School. http://www.angelfire.com/wi/writingprocess/editing.html

Lunsford, A. A. (2005). *EasyWriter* (3rd ed.). Bedford/St.Martins.

Lyons, K. (2005). *Write a literature review*. University of California, Santa Cruz. https://guides.library.ucsc.edu/write-a-literature-review

Martin, D. W. (1991). *Doing psychology experiments* (3rd ed.). Brooks/Cole.

Mathews, B. S. (2004). Gray literature: Resources for locating unpublished research. *College & Research Libraries News, 65*(3), 125–129. https://doi.org/10.5860/crln.65.3.125

McCarthy, M., & Pusateri, T. P. (2006). Teaching students to use electronic databases. In W. Buskist & S. F. Davis (Eds.), *Handbook of the teaching of psychology* (pp. 107–111). Blackwell. https://doi.org/10.1002/9780470754924.ch18

McCormick, K. (1994). On a topic of your own choosing. In J. Clifford & J. Schilb (Eds.), *Writing theory and critical theory* (pp. 33–52). Modern Language Association of America.

McGraw-Hill Higher Education. (n.d.). *How to write term papers*. http://novella.mhhe.com/sites/0079876543/student_view0/research_center-999/research_papers30/how_to_write_term_papers.html

Microsoft. (n.d.). *Get started with OneNote*. https://support.office.com/en-us/article/get-started-with-onenote-e768fafa-8f9b-4eac-8600-65aa10b2fe97?ui=en-US&rs=en-US&ad=US

Miller, G. A. (1956). The magical number seven plus or minus two: Some limits on our capacity for processing information. *Psychological Review, 63*(2), 81–97. https://doi.org/10.1037/h0043158

Miller, H. L., & Lance, C. L. (2006). Written and oral assignments. In W. Buskist & S. F. Davis (Eds.), *Handbook of the teaching of psychology* (pp. 259–264). https://doi.org/10.1002/9780470754924.ch44

Montoya, S. A., Smit, D. J., & Landrum, R. E. (2000, May). *Withdrawals and student transcripts: Do they effect the graduate admissions process?* [Paper presentation]. 73rd Annual Meeting of the Midwestern Psychological Association, Chicago, IL.

Nota Bene. (n.d.). *Nota Bene: Software for academic research & writing*. https://www.notabene.com/chart.html

Obeid, R., & Hill, D. B. (2018). Freely available instructional video and rubric can improve APA style in a research methods classroom. *Scholarship of Teaching and Learning in Psychology, 4*(4), 308–314. https://doi.org/10.1037/stl0000123

Online Writing Laboratory. (n.d.). *Tips and examples for writing thesis statements*. Purdue University. https://owl.purdue.edu/owl/general_writing/the_writing_process/thesis_statement_tips.html

Pennebaker, J. W., Kiecolt-Glaser, J. K., & Glaser, R. (1988). Disclosure of traumas and immune function: Health implications for psychotherapy. *Journal of Consulting and Clinical Psychology, 56*(2), 239–245. https://doi.org/10.1037/0022-006X.56.2.239

Peterson, T. C., Kleppner, S. R., & Botham, C. M. (2018). Ten simple rules for scientists: Improving your writing productivity. *PLOS Computational Biology, 14*(10), e1006379. https://doi.org/10.1371/journal.pcbi.1006379

Pinker, S. (2014, September 26). *Why academics stink at writing*. The Chronicle of Higher Education. https://www.chronicle.com/article/Why-Academics-Writing/148989

Plonsky, M. (2006). *Psychology with style: A hypertext writing guide*. University of Wisconsin—Stevens Point. https://www4.uwsp.edu/psych/mp/APA/apa4b.htm

Price, M. (2002). Beyond "Gotcha!": Situating plagiarism in policy and pedagogy. *College Composition and Communication, 54*(1), 88–115. https://doi.org/10.2307/1512103

Reaves, C. (2004, October). *Teaching APA Style to beginners* [Handout]. Best Practices in Teaching Research Methods and Statistics conference, Atlanta, GA.

Robinson, D. (2019). Engaging students on the first day of class: Student-generated questions promote positive course expectations. *Scholarship of Teaching and Learning in Psychology, 5*(3), 183–188. https://doi.org/10.1037/stl0000139

Roediger, H. L. (2007, April). Twelve tips for authors. *APS Observer, 20*(4), 39–41.

Salovey, P. (2000). Results that get results: Telling a good story. In R. J. Sternberg (Ed.), *Guide to publishing in psychology journals* (pp. 121–132). Cambridge University Press. https://doi.org/10.1017/CBO9780511807862.009

Savage, N. (2015). Scientists in the Twitterverse. *Cell, 162*(2), 233–234. https://doi.org/10.1016/j.cell.2015.06.062

Scott, J. M., Koch, R. E., Scott, G. M., & Garrison, S. M. (2002). *The psychology student writer's manual* (2nd ed.). Prentice Hall.

Shadle, S. (2006, December). *Writing and citing workshop.* Center for Teaching and Learning, Boise State University, Boise, ID.

Shertzer, M. (1986). *The elements of grammar.* Collier Books.

Silvia, P. J. (2007). *How to write a lot: A practical guide to productive academic writing.* American Psychological Association.

Slatcher, R. B., & Pennebaker, J. W. (2006). How do I love thee? Let me count the words: The social effects of expressive writing. *Psychological Science, 17*(8), 660–664. https://doi.org/10.1111/j.1467-9280.2006.01762.x

Sleigh, M. J., & Ritzer, D. R. (2020, Spring). Writing a strong resume for robot and human readers. *Eye on Psi Chi, 24*(3), 22–24. https://doi.org/10.24839/2164-9812.Eye24.3.22

Smith, R. A. (2000). Documenting your scholarship: Citations and references. In R. J. Sternberg (Ed.), *Guide to publishing in psychology journals* (pp. 146–158). Cambridge University Press. https://doi.org/10.1017/CBO9780511807862.011

Smyth, J. M., Stone, A. A., Hurewitz, A., & Kaell, A. (1999, April 14). Effects of writing about stressful experiences on symptom reduction in patients with asthma or rheumatoid arthritis: A randomized trial. *Journal of the American Medical Association, 281*(14), 1304–1309. https://doi.org/10.1001/jama.281.14.1304

Social media for scientists. (2018). Editorial. *Nature Cell Biology, 20,* 1329. https://doi.org/10.1038/s41556-018-0253-6

Spencer, S. M. (2020, Spring). Effective cover letters and resumes: The importance of fit before format. *Eye on Psi Chi, 24*(3), 18–21. https://doi.org/10.24839/2164-9812.Eye24.3.18

Stanton, A. L., Danoff-Burg, S., Sworowski, L. A., Collins, C. A., Branstetter, A. D., Rodriguez-Hanley, A., Kirk, S. B., & Austenfeld, J. L. (2002). Randomized, controlled trial of written emotional expression and benefit finding in breast cancer patients. *Journal of Clinical Oncology, 20*(20), 4160–4168. https://doi.org/10.1200/JCO.2002.08.521

Sternberg, R. J. (2000). Titles and abstracts: They only sound unimportant. In R. J. Sternberg (Ed.), *Guide to publishing in psychology journals* (pp. 37–40). Cambridge University Press. https://doi.org/10.1017/CBO9780511807862.004

Sternberg, R. J. (2005). *The psychologist's companion: A guide to scientific writing for students and researchers* (4th ed.). Cambridge University Press.

Strunk, W., Jr., & White, E. B. (1979). *The elements of style* (3rd ed.). Macmillan.

Szuchman, L. (2005). *Writing with style: APA Style made easy* (3rd ed.). Wadsworth.

Texas A&M University. (n.d.). *Revising & proofreading.* University Writing Center. https://writingcenter.tamu.edu/Students/Writing-Speaking-Guides/Alphabetical-List-of-Guides/Revising-Editing/Revising-Proofreading

Trochim, W. M. K. (2001). *Research methods knowledge base* (2nd ed.). Atomic Dog.

University of Arkansas at Little Rock. (n.d.). *Tips for effective proofreading.* University Writing Center. https://ualr.edu/writingcenter/tips-for-effective-proofreading/

University of Maryland University College. (2011). *Paraphrasing your source.* Online Guide to Writing and Reasearch. https://www.umgc.edu/current-students/learning-resources/writing-center/online-guide-to-writing/tutorial/chapter5/ch5-10.html

University of Melbourne. (n.d.). *Literature reviews.* https://unimelb.libguides.com/lit_reviews

University of North Carolina at Chapel Hill. (n.d.). *Editing and proofreading.* Writing Center. https://writingcenter.unc.edu/resources/handouts-demos/citation/editing-and-proofreading

University of Richmond. (n.d.). *Types of writing in psychology.* Writing Center. http://writing2.richmond.edu/writing/wweb/psychology/types.html

University of Washington. (2017). *Writing a psychology literature review.* Psychology Writing Center. https://psych.uw.edu/storage/writing_center/litrev.pdf

Van Wagenen, R. K. (1991). *Writing a thesis: Substance and style.* Prentice Hall.

Vipond, D. (1993). *Writing and psychology: Understanding writing and its teaching from the perspective of composition studies.* Praeger.

Watson, J. B. (1925). *Behaviorism.* People's Institute.

Western Psychological Association. (2020). Poster design. https://westernpsych.org/poster-design/

Zinsser, W. (1988). *Writing to learn.* Harper & Row.

Zinsser, W. (2008). *On writing well: The classic guide to writing nonfiction* (7th ed.). HarperCollins.

Zou, H., & Hyland, K. (2020). "Think about how fascinating this is": Engagement in academic blogs across disciplines. *Journal of English for Academic Purposes, 43,* 100809. https://doi.org/10.1016/j.jeap.2019.100809

INDEX

ABOUT THE AUTHOR

R. Eric Landrum, PhD, is a professor and chair in the Department of Psychological Science at Boise State University, United States. He received his PhD in cognitive psychology from Southern Illinois University. He is a research generalist, broadly addressing the improvement of teaching and learning, which includes improving the long-term retention of introductory psychology content, skills assessment, help-seeking behavior, and advising innovations, as well as working to understand student career paths, the psychology workforce, successful graduate school applications, and more.

Dr. Landrum has delivered more than 450 presentations, written more than 25 books/textbooks, and published 91 peer-reviewed journal articles in his career to date. He has collaborated with over 325 research assistants and has taught over 18,500 students in 28 years at Boise State. During the summer of 2008, he led an American Psychological Association (APA) working group at the National Conference for Undergraduate Education in Psychology, studying the desired results of an undergraduate psychology education. At the 2014 APA Educational Leadership Conference, Dr. Landrum received a Presidential Citation for outstanding contributions to the teaching of psychology. He also served as an inaugural coeditor of the *Scholarship of Teaching and Learning in Psychology* journal, which launched in 2015. He is a member of APA, a fellow of Division 2 (Society for the Teaching of Psychology) and Division 1 (General Psychology), and he served as Division 2 president in 2014. He is a charter member of the Association for Psychological Science (named fellow in 2018). During 2016–2017, Dr. Landrum was president of the Rocky Mountain Psychological Association and served as president of Psi Chi, the International Honor Society in Psychology, in 2017–2018. In August 2019, he received the

American Psychological Foundation's Charles L. Brewer Distinguished Teaching of Psychology Award, the highest award given to teachers of psychology in America.

Dr. Landrum frequently teaches an Introduction to the Psychology Major course, research methods, and the Capstone Perspectives course, but he has also taught introductory psychology, statistical methods, psychological measurement, learning, and cognitive psychology.